Kohlhammer

About Death Penalty
Reflections on Legal History

From the Code of Hammurabi and Sumerian Precursors up to Germanic Law, the Roman Empire and the Middle Ages

by

Dr. Volker Krey*
Full Professor of Law
State University of Trier, Faculty of Law
Judge at the Court of Appeals, criminal division,
City of Koblenz (1978–1998)

With assistance by:

Stefan Weber (studying Latin and History),
Peter Staudacher (law student), both at Trier University.
Dr. Thomas Roggenfelder, Attorney at Law,
a former member of the staff of the author's chair.

Verlag W. Kohlhammer

Dedicated to my friend and former academic pupil
Prof. Dr. Hans-Ludwig Günther
State University of Tübingen

Gesamtherstellung: W. Kohlhammer GmbH, Stuttgart

Print:
ISBN 978-3-17-036783-8

E-Book-Formate:
pdf: ISBN 978-3-17-036784-5
epub: ISBN 978-3-17-036785-2
mobi: ISBN 978-3-17-036786-9

Table of Contents

Introduction . . . VII

Chapter One: The Code of Hammurabi and Sumerian Precursors . . . 1
I. The most Important Sumerian Precursor: Code of Ur-Nammu . . . 1
1. General Overview. . . . 1
2. Crimes threatened with the Death Penalty . . . 2
3. Contrast to the Code of Hammurabi. . . . 4
4. A brief Summary . . . 4
II. Code of Hammurabi . . . 4
1. General Overview. . . . 4
2. Crimes threatened with the Death Penalty . . . 5
3. Capital Punishment, aggravated in a cruel manner . . . 6
4. Further Cruelties: Corporal Punishment. . . . 7
5. Reasons for the Cruelty of Hammurabi's Code . . . 7

Chapter Two: Germanic Law and Roman Law . . . 9
III. Germanic Law . . . 9
1. General Characterization of the Germanic Law. . . . 9
2. Predominance of Private Criminal Law: Criminal Law as a Private Matter . . . 10
3. Beginning of Public Criminal Law. . . . 11
IV. Roman Law . . . 11
1. Roman Republic . . . 12
a) Private Criminal Law and the Law of the Twelve Tables . . . 12
b) coercitio. . . . 14
c) tresviri capitales . . . 14
d) leges iudiciorum publicorum . . . 14
e) leges iudiciorum publicorum: no Enactment of the Principle "nulla poena sine lege" . . . 15
f) Conclusion. . . . 17
2. Roman Imperial Era . . . 18
3. Outlook . . . 19

Chapter Three: The Early Middle Ages . . . 21
V. Beginning and End of this Era. . . . 21
VI. Extent and Importance of the Frankish Empire . . . 22
VII. Legal Sources and Nature of the Frankish Law . . . 23
1. Legal Sources. . . . 23
2. The very Nature of the Frankish Law . . . 24
VIII. About the Criminal Law of the Frankish Kingdom. . . . 25
1. Frankish Criminal Law in its core being Private Criminal Law . . . 25

2. Elements of Public Criminal Law within the Law of the Frankish Kingdom . . . 26
3. Implications for the Nature of the Early Middle Ages . . . 27

Chapter Four: The High Middle Ages . . . 29
IX. The Beginning and End of the High Middle Ages. Delimitation between this Era and the Late Middle Ages as well as the Early Modern Age . . . 29
1. The Beginning of the High Middle Ages . . . 29
2. The End of the High Middle Ages: An Overview of this Problem . . . 29
3. The Author's Position on the Delimitation of the High Middle Ages . . . 31
X. General Assessment of the High Middle Ages . . . 32
1. Continuing Predominance of Private Criminal Law . . . 32
2. The "Gottesfrieden" (Peace and Truce of God) and "Landfrieden" (Public Peace) as Instruments to restrict Feuds . . . 32
XI. First Steps towards Public Criminal Law including Death Penalty . . . 33
1. Threat of Punishment for Cases of breaking the Ban of Violence laid down in applicable "Landfrieden" . . . 33
2. Heresy Trials: Role Model for Public Criminal Law with Burning and Torturing not until the Late Middle Ages . . . 33
3. The Rise of Cities with autonomous Town Statutes: No Development of Criminal Law striking Life and Limb associated with Torture during the High Middle Ages . . . 33

Chapter Five: A brief Outlook for the Late Middle Ages . . . 35
XII. Beginning and gradual Increase of the cruel "Inqisitionsprozess" ex officio characterized by Torture and Death Penalty during the Late Middle Ages . . . 35
1. The Role of the Church . . . 35
2. The Role of northern Italian cities and German ones . . . 36
3. Beginning of bloodthirsty Witch Trials . . . 36
4. The Role of the German Territorial Princes . . . 36
5. The "Sachsenspiegel" . . . 37
XIII. Hexenbulle and Hexenhammer: Major Blots with strong Impact on the Waves of Witch Trials during the first two Centuries of the Early Modern Age . . . 37
1. The Papal Bull "Summis Desiderantes" (in German "Hexenbulle" i.e. bull on witches) . . . 37
2. Kramer's combat writing "Malleus Maleficarum" ("Hexenhammer" i.e. witch hammer) . . . 37

Introduction

During the period of the *vorstaatlichen Gesellschaften* (pre-state societies), meaning the *hunters and gatherers* as well as the *pre-state segmental societies*[1], in principle there was no legal order and thus no criminal law. Of course, there already existed a large number of unwritten behavioural norms being part of the **pre-legal** social order, such as incest taboo, prohibition of stealing hunting weapons of another Horde/clan member,[2] and last but not least the taboo of killing those members. Furthermore, in cases of serious **infringements of such prohibitions** respectively **breaking taboos**, there obviously were informal mechanisms for conflict-resolution, such as negotiations, e.g. ending by agreements about compensation to the person concerned respectively about the offender leaving the Horde.[3] By contrast, because there was no criminal law at that time, all the more death penalty against offenders in principle was unknown; this even held true in case of homicide.[4]

Certainly, there have been cases of blood revenge.[5] However, such reactions were very dangerous to the domestic peace, because blood revenge could lead to blood feuds being characterized by **mutual bloodshed within the circle of retaliatory revenge.**[6] Thus, blood revenge in principle was not at all in the interest of the Horde/clan, therefore unwanted and unusual.[7]

Rather, the most serious sanction for intolerable misdeeds may have been the **exclusion of the offender from society,** provided that it was necessary for the community's security and domestic peace.[8]

The mentioned informal mechanisms for conflict resolution within those pre-state societies may have been based on the prevailing principle of equality among the members of such Horde; those societies were to be characterized as authority-free, non-hierarchical.[9] Thus, in the absence of a ruler, there was no one equipped with the authority to impose death penalty against a member of the Horde. In contrast, where a community has got a ruler, e.g. a tribal chief or even a king, typically the temptation arose to increase his power. And after all, one characteristic part of the power of a community chief increasingly became the domination over life and death.

Hence, the development of death penalty in principle was to be expected not before the time when communities like tribes respectively city states have got leaders and so lost the nature as authority-free societies.

---

1 As to this period see Wesel, Geschichte des Rechts, 4th edition, 2014, side note 5, 6 et seq., 18 et seq.

2 These examples are named by Wesel, side note 11, 15.

3 Wesel (supra note 1), side note 7, 8, 14, 27, 29.

4 See Wesel, side note 7, 8, 14, 15, 27, 29. To this, Wesel nowhere mentions death penalty, but only the aforesaid informal mechanisms for conflict-resolution in serious cases like homicide.

5 Wesel, side note 27.

6 Thereto (regarding Germanic Law) Krey, Interrogational Torture in Criminal Proceedings – Reflections on Legal History –, Vol. I, in: Rechtspolitisches Forum (Legal Policy Forum), Institut für Rechtspolitik (IRP), University of Trier, No 68, dated 2014, p. 19–22; Krey, About Magicians and Witches – Reflections on Legal History – from the Ancient World up to the High Middle Ages, in: Festschrift for Walter Lindacher (C.H.Beck, Munich, publication 2017), p. 235, 237, 238 at the end, 239; both with further references.

7 Wesel, side note 27 at the end. The undesirability and rarity of blood revenge due to its aforesaid hazardous nature also held true for the mentioned period of Germanic Law; see Krey (supra note 6).

8 Regarding the hunters and gatherers see Wesel (supra note 1), side note 7, 8, 14.

9 Thereto Wesel, side note 8, 14, 22, 34.

Chapter One: **The Code of Hammurabi and Sumerian Precursors**

1 The Code of *Hammurabi*[10], circa 1700 B.C., was the first **largely comprehensive codification** within the Near East (*Vorderer Orient*). This code consists of 282 legal regulations (articles) concerning predominantly civil law and, to a quarter, **criminal law.** Still today, *Hammurabi's* code has often been characterized as the oldest known codification of mankind. However, there are Sumerian precursors. So, the author will start with some remarks on such a precursor.

I. The most Important Sumerian Precursor: Code of Ur-Nammu

1. General Overview

2 At the beginning of the 3rd millennium B.C. the development of the first Sumerian cities Rtook place, and this occurred in the south of Mesopotamia, situated between the rivers Euphrates and Tigris.[11] Here, the first **states** arose, characterized with attributes of statehood like a city ruler, a public administration, and municipal law. Such law already was written down, namely on clay tablets with cuneiform script (in German: *Keilschrift*). Thus, one should not talk about a **mere transition to statehood** when discussing the early Sumerian city states.[12]

a) Around 2100 B.C., the so called Code of *Ur-Nammu* was created. This law, discovered in 1948, nowadays is denoted as the **oldest codification** of mankind, the wording of which became known.[13] *Ur-Nammu*, the then-ruling King of ***Ur*** (being an important Sumerian city state at that time) has been designated as the creator of that code. Unfortunately, there is no complete copy (complete version) of his code – in contrast to the Code of *Hammurabi*. Compared with the latter, the preserved parts of *Ur-Nammu's* Code consist of much less regulations than *Hammurabi's* one.[14]
However, in equal measure as later on the Code of *Hammurabi*, already *Ur-Nammu's* Code started with a prologue, praising the king as being the creator of justice and welfare for the poor and the weak on order of the gods.[15]

b) As regards the preserved criminal law provisions (Art.) of *Ur-Nammu's* Code,[16] the following hints shall be sufficient:

(1) The Code of ***Ur-Nammu***, being around 400 years older than *Hammurabi's* one, appears much more ancient than the latter. Obviously, the transition from the old private criminal law to public criminal justice still was not completed at that time.[17] This may be illustrated by the fact, that there still were private sanctions like monitory compensation (punitive damages) instead of criminal punishment in cases of offences like bodily injury, accusation of sorcery, accusing a married woman of adultery, damage to someone else's field (farmland). The code's respective provisions read as follows:

---

10 6th King of Babylon, the so called Old-Babylonian Empire.

11 Regarding the following text see Wesel (supra note 1), side note 32, 50 et seq.

12 Insofar questionable Wesel, side note 67.

13 See Wesel (supra note 1), side note 54 et seq.

14 A little more than 30 regulations (articles); see the text below, b).

15 Wesel, side note 55, 56. As regards **historical sources** see below, footnote 16.

16 The historical **sources** for the code's articles are inter alia cited in Google: The Code of Ur-Nammu, Wikipedia (English); The Ur-Nammu law code – Realhistoryww; both in the august 2017 version.

17 Wesel (supra note 1), side note 64.

18. *If a man knocks out the eye of another man, he shall weigh out ½ a mina of silver.*
19. *If a man has cut off another man's foot, he is to pay ten shekels.*
20. *If a man, in the course of a scuffle, smashed the limb of another man with a club (a mace), he shall pay one mina of silver*
21. *If someone severed the nose of another man with a copper knife, he must pay two-thirds of a mina of silver.*
22. *If a man knocks out a tooth of another man, he shall pay two shekels of silver.*
31. *If a man flooded the field of a man with water, he shall measure out three kur (apparently a unit of measurement) of barley per iku (apparently a square measure) of field.*

Such provisions illustrate that the code's penal law still was shaped by private criminal justice.

However, the urgent question that arises here is the following one: What happened to those perpetrators, who were absolutely unable to pay the respective compensations (punitive damages)? Presumably, the consequences for such perpetrators would be unpleasant.

(2) The mentioned regulations of *Ur-Nammu's* Code for *accusation of sorcery* respectively for *accusing a married woman of adultery* say:

13. *If a man is accused of sorcery, he must undergo ordeal by water, if he is proven innocent,*[18] *his accuser must pay three shekels.*

Here, it seems surprising, that the penalty for the offender of such a serious crime as being regulated in the Code's Art. 13 was so lenient, although that accusation was absolutely life-threatening for the accused victim concerned. In contrast, the Code of *Hammurabi* ordered capital punishment for such cases of accusation.[19]

14. *If a man accused the wife of a man of adultery, and the river ordeal*[20] *proved her innocent, then the man who has accused her must pay one-third of a mina of silver.*

Here again, the threatened punishment is surprisingly lenient, considering the acute danger for the life of the accused woman due to the threatening **water ordeal.**

2. Crimes threatened with the Death Penalty

3 The decisive difference between the Code of *Ur-Nammu's* criminal law and the respective part of *Hammurabi's* Code has been reduced by *Wesel* to the simple formula:

> Hammurabi's Code insofar was much harsher than Ur-Nammu's.[21]

This statement is convincing to a great extent, particularly with regard to the **death penalty:**

In this respect, the Code of *Ur-Nammu* all in all can be characterized as exceptionally lenient because only very few criminal offences should be punished with death, namely the following:

Firstly, **murder** pursuant to Art. 1.

1. *If a man commits a murder, that man must be killed.*

Secondly, **robbery**, Art. 2.

2. *If a man commits a robbery, he will be killed.*

---

18 The **ordeal by water,** being a judgement of God, meant at that time: If the river will seize the accused (i.e.: if he drowned), he was found guilty by the God of the river. However, if the God will consider him innocent he will let him go away unscathed. Thereto e.g.: Wesel, side note 64 at the end; Krey in: Festschrift for Lindacher (supra note 6), p. 236 (regarding the Code of Hammurabi, for which the same applied).

19 Thereto Krey in: Festschrift for Lindacher p. 236; also see the following text, II 2.

20 See supra note 18.

21 Wesel (supra note1), side note 76.

Thirdly, a very **serious case of adultery** committed by a man other than the husband, pursuant to Art. 6.

6. *If a man violates the right of another and deflowers the virgin wife of a young man, they shall kill that male.*

This rule seems astonishing because wives, still being virgins, might be rare. However, the code might have had cases of **child marriages** in mind, where the marriage still was not consummated. Here, the code has considered the deflowering of a **married** virgin by a man other than her husband as a very serious misdeed.

Fourthly, a case of **adultery committed by a wife**, Art. 7.

7. *If the wife of a man followed after another man and he slept with her, they shall slay that woman, but that male shall be set free.*

This provision seems to be extraordinarily misogynist, moreover inconsistent. This is because from the perspective at that time, the criminal offence of adultery, committed by a wife, violates **the right of her husband.** However, such violation has been committed by both, the wife and the adulterer. Therefore, it seems to be inconsistent, that only the wife shall be slayed, whereas the adulterer shall be set free without any punishment.

Furthermore, Art. 7 looks strange for an additional reason: As already mentioned, adultery committed by a wife then was considered as offence against her husband's rights. Therefore, the cuckold consequently should have the right to forgive his wife and so to save her life. Such a regulation also might have been expected because *Ur-Nammu's* Code still was shaped by private criminal justice.[22]

> Here, a reference to the Code of *Hammurabi* may be allowed: On the one hand, Art. 129 of this Code reads:[23]
>
> *Wenn die Ehefrau eines Bürgers beim (Zusammen-)Liegen mit einem anderen Mann ergriffen worden ist, so bindet man sie beide und wirft sie ins Wasser.*
>
> Near translation by the author: If a wife is caught in the very act of committing adultery, both, she and the adulterer, shall be bound with fetters and thrown into the river.
>
> On the other hand, Art. 129 continues:
>
> *Wenn der Herr der Ehefrau (gemeint: ihr Ehemann) seine Ehefrau am Leben lässt, so lässt auch der König seinen Knecht (gemeint: den Ehebrecher) am Leben.*
>
> Near translation by the author: If the **husband** of the wife[24] concerned keeps her alive, the King also keeps the adulterer[25] alive.

Such a private settlement of adultery being a typical relict of the old private criminal law is lacking in *Ur-Nammu's* Code. This holds true even when considering that the Code is not completely preserved, since at least the relevant Art. 7 seems to be fully preserved.

Anyhow, I suspect that there may have been *de jure* or *de facto* a chance for the husband to save the life of his adulterous wife.

> As regards the criminal liability for adultery, an additional information seems to be necessary: A **husband** being unfaithful was never ever punishable for adultery.

22 See the text above, Chapter One, I 1 b (1) with footnote 17.

23 **Source:** Eilers, Codex Hammurabi. Die Gesetzesstele Hammurabis, translated by Wilhelm Eilers (revised version of the 1932 published 5th edition), 2009. The paper at hand follows the version of 2009 and its enumeration of the Code's articles (Art.).

24 Hammurabi's Code here designated him as "master of his wife".

25 Hammurabi's Code here called him "the king's servant".

3. Contrast to the Code of Hammurabi

4 As will be shown below,[26] the Code of *Hammurabi* in numerous criminal law provisions has stipulated capital punishment, and in addition often has aggravated such punishment by torturous methods like burning or death by impaling.
By contrast, pursuant to ***Ur-Nammu's* code** only very few criminal offences should be punished with death, and in addition, there were no barbaric methods of capital punishment like burning or impaling to death ordered *expressis verbis*.

However, that fact does not necessarily mean that there were no barbaric penalties as the mentioned ones, but we don't know. Anyhow, a typical method of executing the death penalty might have been **drowning in the river.**[27]

4. A brief Summary

5 Firstly, the Code of *Ur-Nammu* with its very few Articles is far away from any codification of the law. This particularly holds true for the criminal law provisions.
Secondly, there are very few cases of crimes, for which death penalty was stipulated.
Thirdly, there is no case of barbaric forms of executing the capital punishment like burning or impaling to death, being *expressis verbis* ordered in such code.
Fourthly, the ancient criminal law principle "an eye for an eye, a tooth for a tooth" (*lex talionis*, meaning the law of talion, in German: *Talionsprinzip*) can be found in *Ur-Nammu's* Code only in its Art. 1 (death penalty for murder). In contrast, this principle particularly did not apply to the above cited provisions of this Code on bodily injury (Art. 18 to Art. 22).
Fifth, such Code is anything but bloodthirsty; rather, in total it is lenient.
All of this distinguishes Ur-*Nammu's* Code significantly from the later **Code of *Hammurabi*** which shall be discussed in the following.

II. Code of Hammurabi

1. General Overview

6 The Code of *Hammurabi*,[28] coming from the Age of the Old Babylonian Empire, was the first largely comprehensive codification. This Code is engraved on a more than human-sized diorite stele which was discovered at the beginning of the 20th century. It starts with the so-called prologue and ends with the epilogue, denominating inter alia the **purposes** intended by *Hammurabi's* Code as follows:[29]
Firstly, on behalf of the Gods, introducing law and justice.
Regarding this purpose, the **prologue** states e.g.:[30]
Als Marduk (assyrischer Gott) mich beauftragte, die Menschen gerecht zu leiten und dem Land Ordnung zuzuweisen, habe ich Recht und Gerechtigkeit in den Mund des Landes gelegt ...Ich, Hammurabi, ...der das Recht verwirklichte.
Near translation by the author: *When the God Marduk mandated me, to lead the people justly und to impose law and order in my kingdom, I laid down law and justice, accessible for the country ... me, Hammurabi, who realized justice.*

---

26 Chapter One, II 2.

27 This at least applied for the execution of death penalty pursuant to Hammurabi's code. See below, II 2.

28 **Source**: Eilers (supra note 23). **Secondary literature**: see inter alia Eilers, p. 7–17, 18–25; Wesel (supra note 1), side note 68 et seq.; also see Krey, Interrogational Torture in Criminal Proceedings. Reflections on Legal History, Vol. I (supra note 6), p. 14–18; Krey, Keine Strafe ohne Gesetz. Einführung in die Dogmengeschichte des Satzes nullum crimen, nulla poena sine lege (Publishing Company de Gruyter, Berlin), 1983, side note 4, 5, 12, 123.

29 Source Eilers. Secondary literature: see inter alia Krey, Interogational Torture (supra note 28), p. 14, 15; Krey, Keine Strafe ohne Gesetz (supra note 28), side note 4, 5; Wesel, side note 69.

30 See Eilers, p. 27 et seq., 30 and 31.

In addition to this, the **epilogue** inter alia says:[31]
Rechtssprüche der Gerechtigkeit, die Hammurabi, der tüchtige König festgesetzt hat,... Worte der Gerechtigkeit, die ich auf meinen Denkstein (gemeint: die erwähnte Diorit Stele) geschrieben habe ... Hammurabi, der König der Gerechtigkeit ..., dem der Gott Marduk sein Volk anvertraut hat.
Near translation by the author: Legal regulations pursuant to justice, carried out by Hammurabi, the competent King, ... words of justice, I have written down on this diorite stele ... Hammurabi, the King of Justice ... to whom Marduk has entrusted the people.
Secondly, *den Ruchlosen und den Bösen zu vernichten* (i.e. eliminating the nefarious and evil ones).[32]
This purpose might have been one of the reasons for the character of the Code's criminal law as bloodthirsty and cruel, which will be discussed below.[33]
Thirdly, protection of socially deprived persons.
As regards such purpose, the Code states inter alia:
Der Codex bezwecke auch, vom Starken den Schwachen nicht entrechten zu lassen (prologue), ihm sowie der Witwe und Waise Recht zu verschaffen (epilogue).[34]
Near translation by the author: *The Code also had the purpose to ensure that the deprived shall not be disenfranchised by powerful ones, and to give justice to widows, orphans, and disenfranchised people.*

> Such social element as one of the Code's purposes is confirmed inter alia by several provisions on socially acceptable prices and wages[35], e.g. Art. 258, 261, 269, 272.[36]

Additionally, *Hammurabi's* Code in its epilogue emphasized:
*Der **entrechtete** Bürger ... trete vor mein Bildnis "König der Gerechtigkeit"*[37] *und lese meinen Schriftstein ... und mein Denkstein kläre ihm seinen Rechtshandel ...*
Near translation by the author: *The **disenfranchised** citizen shall come before my effigy*[38] *as King of justice and there shall read my Code engraved on the diorite stele, which may explain to him the legal case concerned.*

2. Crimes threatened with the Death Penalty

The penal provisions of *Hammurabi's* Code include numerous Articles covering a wide range of classic penal law. A great many of these penal provisions ordered the use of the **death penalty**; here, in particular the following types of such criminal offences ought to be named:[39] 7

Art. 1 False accusation of murder
Art. 2 False accusation of sorcery[40]
Art. 3 False accusation before a court responsible for capital crimes
Art. 6 Theft (and receiving) of property of the temple respectively of the King/royal court

31 Eilers, p. 91 et seq., 92, 93.
32 Eilers, p. 27.
33 Thereto the following text, II 2.
34 See Eilers, p. 27 (prologue) and 92 (epilogue).
35 This is also pointed out by Wesel (supra note 1), side note 69.
36 Regarding inter alia: wage for a farm labourer taking care of cattle (Art. 258); wage for a herdsman who let the cattle and/or small domestic animals graze (Art. 261); payment for rent a donkey (Art. 269); payment for rent a cart (Art. 272).
37 Meaning the picture of Hammurabi engraved on the top of the diorite stele, on which his Code is engraved.
38 See supra note 37.
39 Source: see supra note 23. Already see Krey, Interrogational Torture Vol. I (supra note 6), p.15 footnote 14.
40 Thereto Krey in Festschrift for Lindacher (supra note 6), p. 236.

Art. 14 Deprivation of liberty (kidnapping) against the "little son" of a citizen
Art. 15 Allowing/helping servants of the King/royal court or of citizens to escape
Art. 16 Hiding of escaped servants of the King/royal court in spite of the herald's calling
Art. 21 Burglary into a house/home – *death by hanging* –
Art. 22 Robbery
Art. 25 Theft in case of using a fire – *death by burning* –
Art. 26 A soldier's refusal to obey an order to participate in a military campaign of the king
Art. 34 Theft committed by military leaders against subordinated soldiers
Art. 108 Fraudulent conducts leading to overcharged prices committed by **female** innkeepers when selling beer – *death by drowning* –
Art. 109 A female innkeeper, in whose house fraudsters have gathered, fails to betray them to the King
Art. 110 *Naditu*-priestess or *Entu*-priestess, living outside of a monastery, opens the entrance door to an inn (pub) or even enters in order to have a beer – *death by burning* –
Art. 129 Adultery, unless the husband of the adulterous wife keeps her alive (as already discussed above)[41] – *death by drowning* –
Art. 130 Rape of a citizen's wife who still has been a virgin before that criminal offence and still was living in her father's house[42]
Art. 143 A wife, not being respectable, who regularly leaves the house, squanders the households appliances, and neglects her husband, shall be *drowned*
Art. 153 A wife's instigation to murder her husband for another man – *death by impaling* –
Art. 155 Sexual intercourse with the wife of his son, if the latter already had slept with her – *death by drowning* –
Art. 157 Sexual intercourse of a man with his mother after his father's death – *both shall be killed by burning* –
Art. 209 in connection with Art. 210: Beating the pregnant daughter of a citizen, resulting in the loss of her foetus and the daughter's death – *punishment of the offender by killing his own daughter instead of him* –

For clarification: This penal provision illustrates the *lex talionis*[43] (here, *a life for a life*), in a terrible connection with clan liability in its appearance: *the life of your daughter for the life of my daughter.*[44]

Art. 229 If a contractor has built a house not being stable enough and which therefore has collapsed resulting in the house owner's death, such contractor shall be killed.
Art. 230 If the house owner's son has been killed by the collapse of that house the son of its constructor shall be killed.

This Article as well illustrates the mentioned connection of the *lex talionis* with clan liability, here saying: *the life of your son for the life of my son.*

3. Capital Punishment, aggravated in a cruel manner

8 In addition, the outlined frequent use of capital punishment was made even worse by the fact that in many cases such punishment was **aggravated in a cruel manner**, namely by *burning to death* or by *impaling* as already mentioned.[45]

41 See the text above, I 2 with footnote 23–25.
42 As to **a wife as virgin** see above Chapter One, I 2, thirdly (regarding Art. 6 of Ur-Nammu's Code).
43 See the text above, I 4.
44 A further example for this provides Art. 230 of Hammurabi's Code (see the text below).
45 Thereto the aforesaid Articles 25, 110, 157 (burning), 153 (impaling).

4. Further Cruelties: Corporal Punishment

Finally, there were numerous cases of awful *bodily mutilation* respectively *whipping/ flogging* ordered by *Hammurabi's* Code, both penalties also being elements of a cruel criminal law.[46] 9

Here, particularly the following penalties on the offender concerned ought to be named:

- Cutting off his tongue (Art. 192)
- Pulling out or destroying in other ways one of his eyes (Art. 193, 196)
- Cutting off the breast of a female offender (Art. 194)
- Cutting off one of his hands (Art. 195, 218)
- Breaking a bone of his (Art. 197)

  In this context, often the *lex talionis*[47] is involved (Art. 196, 197, in addition Art. 200).
- Whipping/flogging by 60 lashes with a whip (Art. 202)[48], being awful and life threatening.

5. Reasons for the Cruelty of Hammurabi's Code

Wesel describes *Hammurabi's* criminal law as "bloodthirsty", and rightly so; in this context, he states: *as regards the reasons for such blood lust one only could speculate.*[49] However, in my opinion there are some grounds, at least being plausible: 10

Firstly, the cruelty of this criminal law might have aimed at replacing private revenge, in particular blood vengeance, clan feud and generally private criminal law by means of the predominance of public criminal law.

For such purpose, it might be helpful to carry out a harsh criminal law which meets the victim's respectively his relatives' desire for getting satisfaction.[50]

Secondly, *Hammurabi's* criminal law also was so terribly harsh, because his Code carried the authority of this mighty King in his capacity as **supreme ruler of justice.** Thus, serious breaches of his penal provisions might have been considered as contempt of his authority, so to say as **crime against the crown.**

Thirdly, as already mentioned, the prologue and epilogue of *Hammurabi's* Code praise the King as representative of the Gods with the divine mandate to create justice among the people: The Gods had chosen him to be King of Righteousness. Therefore, serious breaches of the Code's penal provisions at the same time were acts of sacrilege against the Gods.

---

46 Krey, Interrogational Torture (supra note 6), p. 16 with footnote 18, 19.
47 Thereto the text above, Chapter One, I 4, II 2 at the end.
48 See Krey (supra note 46), p. 16 footnote 19.
49 Wesel (supra note 1), side note 76.
50 Concerning the text above see Krey (supra note 46), p. 17, 18.

Chapter Two: **Germanic Law and Roman Law**

III. Germanic Law

The age of Germanic Law[51] is traditionally described as the time between the epoch of the barbarian migration into the Western Roman Empire (as to the third century A.D.) and the age of the Kingdom of the Francs (since the end of the fifth century A.D.). **11**

However, it must be acknowledged that Germanic tribes, namely the *Cimbri* and *Teutons* had invaded the Roman Empire already at the end of the second century B.C., but finally were eliminated by the Roman commander *Marius*.[52]

Due to lack of written culture in the days of the ancient Germanic tribes, there are only a few written **sources** relating to the Germanic Law.
The most important one may be the famous "*Germania*" of *Tacitus*, a Roman senator and historian (58–120 A.D.); this paper, being an ethnological monograph, dated at the end of the first century A.D.[53] Yet, when assessing the reliability of *Tacitus's* statements, one has to take the following into consideration: *Tacitus* has idealized the Germanic people in order to confront the degenerated Roman society with a counter-image.[54]
Further important sources are the tribal laws *(leges barbarorum)*, applying to the different Germanic tribes who lived under the rule of the Kingdom of the Franks.[55] Here, the *Lex Salica*, being the tribal law of the Franks as the reigning tribe, has to be pointed out at the first place. This tribal law, enacted by the Frankish King *Chlodwig* at the beginning of the 6th century A.D., still was decisively influenced by Germanic legal traditions.[56]
Finally, the Icelandic Sagas (Sagas of Icelanders)[57] relating to the early time of the settlement of Iceland should be mentioned here. This is because they described the life of the emigrants from Norway to Island at a time being without any relevant influence by Christianity and/or Roman law and therefore reflecting old Germanic traditions.[58]

1. General Characterization of the Germanic Law

As regards this issue, the author can refer to some of his former publications.[59] **12**
The relevant insights and views stated there shall be reproduced here, but in an abbreviated version where possible and appropriate. The same applies to the issues, discussed under the points 2. and 3. hereafter.

---

51 As regards this age see inter alia Wesel, side note 175–184; also see: Gmür/Roth, Grundriss der Deutschen Rechtsgeschichte, 11th edition 2006, side note 19–30; Krey, Interrogational Torture in Criminal Proceedings (supra note 6), p. 19–24, and Krey, About Magicians and Witches ..., in: Festschrift for Lindacher (supra note 6), p. 237–240; Rüping/Jerouschek, Grundriss der Strafrechtsgeschichte, 6th edition, 2011, side note 1–7.

52 Thereto: Der Kleine Pauly, Lexikon der Antike, 1979, Vol. 1, keyword Cimbri; Vol. 5, keyword Teutoni. Such invasion may be the reason, why Gmür/Roth date back the beginning of the Germanic Epoch to 100 B.C.

53 Thereto inter alia: Gmür/Roth (supra note 51), side note 20, 24, 26, 30; Krey, About Magicians und Witches (supra note 6), p. 237; Rüping/Jerouschek (supra note 51), side note 2.

54 See footnote 53.

55 Thereto the text below, with footnote 56.

56 See: v. Hippel, Deutsches Strafrecht, Bd. 1, 1925 (reprint 1971), p.109; Krey, p. 237; Wesel (supra note 1), side note 176, 178, 192, and 193.

57 See: The Sagas of Islanders, preface by Jane Smiley, Introduction by Robert Kellog, Penguin Books, 2001.

58 Thereto Rüping/Jerouschek (supra note 51), side note 3.

59 Krey, Interrogational Torture (supra note 6), p. 19 et seq.; Krey, in: Festschrift for Lindacher, p. 237 et seq.

The Germanic Law is characterized by the following legal position of Germanic people, more precisely **freemen** of the respective Germanic tribe in contrast to bondsmen or slaves. Killing a freeman or committing bodily injury against him outside times of war, in principle was regarded as taboo.
In contrast to Roman Law, even slaves were regarded as human beings and not as a thing like animals being mere subjects of property law.[60] Even bondsmen and slaves usually were not subject of legal killing or severe physical ill-treatment at the **discretion** of their master.[61]
Yet, regarding killing or severe maltreating slaves or bondsmen, this paper cannot go into detail.
The outlined idea of man (in German: *Menschenbild*), saying that life and limb of a Germanic freeman in principle were untouchable and therefore had to be respected by the general public (tribal community), led to the following structure of Germanic criminal law:

2. Predominance of Private Criminal Law: Criminal Law as a Private Matter

13 In principle, crimes were private affairs of the clans concerned; hence, crimes did not affect the respective Germanic tribe. Rather, criminal law was a private matter as can be seen below:
a) Interior offences, meaning offences inside of a clan, were punished by the head of the clan. Here, the most serious revenge was the exclusion from the clan leading to the loss of protection by the clan. In contrast, blood vengeance by killing the perpetrator probably was unusual.[62]
b) External crimes, i.e. crimes committed by a member of one clan against a member of another clan, were treated as attack by the perpetrator's clans against the victim's one. So, the reaction was **clan feud**. Such feuds (blood feuds) allowed as a means of blood vengeance the killing of any male member of the offender's clan. This could result in an endless cycle of retaliatory revenge between the clans involved.[63] Thus, clan feuds could lead to considerable casualties among the male members of the clans concerned and therefore were highly undesirable for the affected tribe.[64]
As a consequence, there was the early development of an instrument aiming at replacing clan feuds by providing **blood money**: On the basis of a contract between the offender's clan and the victim's one, the latter could waive the right to blood feud in return for blood money

– offered as an attempt to satisfy the desire for revenge of the victim's clan –.

Such contracts, in German called *Sühneverträge* (i.e. expiation contracts), were often entered into by reason of an intervention by chiefs of the respective tribe. The here stipulated "blood money" (Weregild/Wergild) typically was not rated in money, but in a certain number of horses, cattle, weapons etc.[65]
The mentioned replacement of the right to kill a Germanic freeman in the context of clan feuds due to the acceptance of blood money expressively agreed in an expiation

---

60 Rüping/Jerouschek, side note 4; dissenting, but to some extent too speculative, Eb. Schmidt, Einführung in die Geschichte der deutschen Strafrechtspflege, 3rd edition 1965, p. 26 at the end, 27.

61 See supra note 60.

62 Thereto v. Hippel, Deutsches Strafrecht, Vol. 1, 1925 (reprint 1971), p. 41, 42 with further references; dissenting Eb. Schmidt, p. 26 at the end, 27.

63 See: v. Hippel, p. 40, 41; Eb.Schmidt, p. 22, 23; Wesel (supra note 1), side note 181, 183. Also see the text of the paper at hand, Introduction with footnote 6, 7.
A fact being illustrated particularly in the Icelandic Sagas in an expressive and elaborate manner. Thereto: The Sagas of Icelanders, preface by Jane Smily, introduction by Robert Kellog, Penguin Books, 2001.

64 Already see text above, **Introduction**, with footnote 6, 7.

65 See: Gmür/Roth (supra note 51), side note 20, 24; Rüping/Jerouschek (supra note 51), side note 6; Wesel, side note 181, 183.

contract,[66] probably occurred in numerous cases for otherwise whole tribes could have been eliminated to a significant extent over the decades.
c) At first glance, such development seems to be astonishing because the **right** to start a clan feud and thereby take blood vengeance implied at the same time a **matter of honour** to do so. However, there were good reasons to enter into a *Sühnevertrag*[67] despite such aspects of honour: Firstly, a great extent of the offered Weregild/Wergild;[68] secondly the mentioned influence of intervening tribe chiefs; thirdly cases of a weak power of the victim's clan compared to the offender's one.

3. Beginning of Public Criminal Law

Beside the predominant private criminal law, there was the beginning of public criminal law regarding very serious crimes which affected or endangered the tribe in a significant manner.[69] **14**
Here, *Tacitus* denotes treason and cowardice at war, to be punished by death penalty.[70] Other authors cite cases of sacrilege.[71] However, often the perpetrator's banishment was ordered instead of his execution, indicating that killing a Germanic freeman on behalf of the tribe's authority in principle was undesirable.

Occasionally, as a further example of death penalty under the scarcely developed public criminal law of Germanic tribes the **killing of witches/sorcerers** is referred to.[72] This view seems questionable to me. The reasons for this have been laid down by the author in an earlier publication,[73] to which reference is made here. By the way, it is controversial whether or not the numerous findings of **bog bodies** (in German: *Moorleichen*) dated from the Age of Germanic Law may be taken as proof for the use of death penalty. A widespread opinion states: *here human sacrifices were concerned.*[74] In contrast, *Tacitus* in his "*Germania*" states that in cases of cowardice at war *the perpetrators were sunk in the bog.*[75] Finally, there is the opinion that both was applicable,[76] which seems plausible to me.

IV. Roman Law

As is well known, the Continental European Law, abbreviated as *Continental Law* **15**
– also called *Civil Law*, and this mostly in the field of comparative law and here in contrast to Common Law[77] –

---

66 Thereto Tacitus, Germania, see text above (III. with footnote 53, 54), cited pursuant to Gmür/Roth (supra note 51), side note 20. In addition see v. Hippel (supra note 56), p. 42, 103, and Rüping/Jerouschek (supra note 51), side note 5, 6.
67 See text above, III 2 b).
68 See supra note 67.
69 Thereto: Gmür/Roth, side note 24; v. Hippel, p. 43, 49, 101, 103–105; Eb. Schmidt (supra note 60), p. 25, 29 et seq.; Wesel (supra note 1), side note 183, referring to Tacitus.
70 In: Germania (see text above with footnote 53), chapter 12; also see: v. Hippel, p. 103, 104; Krey, About Magicians and Witches (supra note 6), p. 239; Eb. Schmidt, p. 25; Wesel, side note 183.
71 Thereto: v. Hippel, p. 104 with footnote 9.
72 References for this point of view in: Krey (supra note 70), p. 239, 240.
73 Krey, About Magicians and Witches (supra note 6), p. 239, 240 with further references.
74 Thereto Rüping/Jerouschek (supra note 51), side note 7.
75 See supra note 70; quoted from Gmür/Roth (supra note 51), side note 20.
76 Apparently alike Rüping/Jerouschek, side note 7.
77 The latter terminology "Civil Law" seems implausible because misleading: Here, the important difference between Criminal Law and **Civil Law/Private Law** in the sense of Law of Contracts, Law of Torts, and Commercial Law etc. is neglected, since naturally also in the field of Continental Law there is such private law **and** criminal law.

has been influenced to a great extent by the Roman Law, namely through the so called Reception of such law.[78] Primarily, this is true for private law but to a significant extent for criminal law as well.[79] Regarding that Reception of Roman Law, the following brief hints shall be sufficient:[80]
In the course of the foundation of the first universities since the end of the 11th century (Bologna etc.), Canon Law/Ecclesiastical Law and the rediscovered Roman Law pursuant to the *Corpus Juris Justinian's*[81] became the subject matter of Law Studies. In this way, the so-called Reception of Roman Law started throughout Europe.

1. Roman Republic

16 As regards this issue, the author can refer to some of his former publications[82] to a certain extent. So, relevant insights and views stated there shall be reproduced here, but in an abbreviated version where possible and appropriate. This also applies to the issues discussed under points **2.**, and **3.** hereafter.

Such era started with the expulsion of the last king (about 500 B.C.) and ended 27 B.C. with the beginning of the Principate of *Augustus*.

17 **a) Private Criminal Law and the Law of the Twelve Tables.** Law at that time initially was customary law, applied by members of the upper class (patricians) and thereby concealed from the members of the lower class (plebeians).
However, soon after the establishment of the Roman Republic, the plebeians achieved that essential parts of the law were laid down by statute law, namely in the famous Law of the Twelve Tables (in Latin: *Leges Duodecim Tabularum*), dated 451 B.C. This statute law aimed at restricting arbitrariness of the judges from the upper class.[83]
(1) Long after the promulgation of such statute law, there still was private criminal law to a significant extent, as shown below:[84]
Within the family, the *pater familias* (i.e. the head of the family) was holder of the penal power up to the *"ius vitae ac necis"* (i.e. power of life and death).[85] However, **de facto** this power of life and death did not play an important role. More relevant might have been the head of the family's power to impose the banishment of the respective offender, e.g. his son, from Rome.[86] Furthermore, the aforesaid power of life and death was limited by the *"mos maiorum"* (i.e. the custom of the ancestors),[87] monitored and – in case of serious offences – sanctioned by the Roman Censor.
External crimes as well have long been to a great extent a **private matter.** For example, in certain cases such as theft nocturnal or adultery, the victim was allowed to kill the

---

78 Fried, Das Mittelalter, 2nd edition 2009, p. 110, 111, 195, 196, 232 et seq.; v. Hippel (supra note 56), p. 90, 91, 159 et seq.; Rüping/Jerouschek (supra note 51), side note 29, 30–34; Wesel (supra note 1), side note 202, 215–217.

79 Thereto inter alia: v. Hippel, p. 159 et seq., 163 et seq.; Rüping/Jerouschek, side note 30 et seq., 34, 85 et seq., 94 et seq., 96, 97; also see Wesel, side note 237, 239, 240, 246.

80 Already see: Krey, Interrogational Torture, Volume I (supra note 6), p. 43; Krey, About Magicians and Witches (supra note 6), p. 247.

81 Published in 533, 534 A.D.

82 Krey, Interrogational Torture, Volume I (supra note 6), p. 25–33; Krey, About Magicians and Witches (supra note 6), p. 240–243.

83 Krey, Keine Strafe ohne Gesetz (supra note 28), side note 4, 9 with further references; Wesel (supra note 1), side note 131.

84 Thereto: v. Hippel (supra note 56), p. 55 et seq.; Mommsen, Römisches Strafrecht, 1899 (reprint 1961), p. 54 to 64; Wesel, side note 133.

85 v. Hippel, p. 55; also see Mommsen, p. 16 et seq.

86 v. Hippel, p. 55; Mommsen, p. 23.

87 v. Hippel, p. 55 footnote 3.

offender caught in the very act.[88] Moreover, acts of revenge for the most part were replaced by entering into *"Sühneverträge"* (i.e. expiation contracts).[89]
(2) Nevertheless, the Law of the Twelve Tables had enacted criminal law provisions to a certain extent and thereby stipulated capital punishment for a few offences such as nocturnal theft of harvest, arson, false testimony.[90] In this context, a relevant statement of *Cicero* shall be quoted, saying:

The death penalty was threatened only "in very few cases".[91]

(3) Regarding *parricidium* (i.e. **intentional killing**), there was a strange mixture between elements of private criminal law on the one hand and elements of public criminal law on the other hand during the first centuries of the Roman Republic. Such capital crime was worthy of capital punishment and considered as offence against the community.[92] **18**
Nevertheless, the murderer's fate in principle was in the hands of the **victim's family/clan** at that time:
If a criminal court had declared the murderer guilty he was handed over to that family/clan in order to enable private revenge.[93] In such case, the aforesaid family/clan could kill the offender or sell him into slavery.[94] But instead of those acts of revenge, there was for a long time during the early republic the often or even mostly used solution by *"taking blood money in return for the waiver of revenge"*.[95]
Furthermore, where perpetrators, charged with *parricidium*, must face the imposition and execution of death penalty, in principle they could evade this punishment by going into **banishment** (in Latin: *exilium*).[96]

(4) Summing up, during the early Roman Republic (its first and second century), there was no significant relevance of death penalty; this is true at least for Roman Citizens. **19**

In addition, only very rarely a corporal punishment like mutilation and whipping was ordered by the Law of the Twelve Tables.[97]

The reasons for this might have been the following: The **idea of man** (in German: *Menschenbild*) as for the Roman Citizens saying that life and limb in principle were untouchable and therefore had to be respected by the public authority, might have led to the result that death penalty as well as mutilation and whipping were undesirable.[98]

---

88 v. Hippel, p. 56 at the end, 57 with footnote 1.

89 v. Hippel, p. 57; Wesel, side note 133.

90 See Düll, Das Zwölftafelgesetz, 3rd edition 1959, p. 51, 55.

91 Thereto Düll, p. 48.

92 See v. Hippel (supra note 56), p. 59–61; Mommsen (supra note 84), p. 612 et seq., 939, 940.

93 Wesel (supra note 1), side note 133.

94 Wesel, side note 133.

95 See text above, IV 1 a (1) with footnote 89.

96 Thereto: v. Hippel, p. 60, 68; Mommsen, p. 922, 923, 941 et seq.

97 As regards **mutilation**, the Twelve Tables (Table VIII, 2) ordered: "If someone mutilates a limb (of another person) he shall suffer the same evil unless there is an amicable arrangement between the offender and the victim concerned". Near translation into English by the author.
Concerning **whipping**, such punishment applied to Roman Citizens only in one exceptional case pursuant to the Twelve Tables (Table VIII, 14 – according to Gellius), saying: "... ordered by the Decemviri (meaning the authors of the first Ten Tables) against a thief caught in the very act that such an offender if he was a Roman Citizens was flagellated and given as a slave to the victim". Near translation into English by the author.
Already see Krey, Interrogational Torture, Volume I (supra note 6), p. 25–27 with further references.

98 Alike Krey, p. 25–27; likewise already: v. Hippel, p. 60, 62, 65 with footnote 4, 68; Mommsen (supra note 84), p. 922, 923, 941, 981.

Here, a clear parallel between the idea of man regarding **Roman Citizens** and the idea of man concerning **Germanic freemen**[99] should be noted.

20 **b) coercitio.** Besides the penal power of public criminal courts there was the so called *coercitio* meaning the **coercive power** of supreme state authorities (Roman consuls and praetors). Such competence included an extensive penal power even covering bodily punishment and death penalty.[100] This legal situation created the danger of intolerable arbitrariness. Hence, such *ius vitae ac necis*[101] quite soon was restricted by the affected Roman Citizens' right of appeal to the people (in Latin: *provocatio ad populum*) in case of capital punishment by coercive power.[102]

In addition, but at a later date, the mentioned Roman state authorities' right to impose corporal punishment against Roman citizens in principle was set aside.[103]

21 **c) tresviri capitales.** Since the third century B.C., a specific criminal court called *tresviri capitales* was established in order to fight the mass crime committed in Rome, meanwhile a city of several hundred thousand inhabitants.[104] This court allowing brief and dashing criminal trials apparently was competent for slaves and members of the lower class. Here, depending on the severity of the criminal offence in question, e.g. intentional fire-raising and burglary, even death penalty was applicable.[105]

22 **d) leges iudiciorum publicorum.** During the late Roman Republic, namely since the second century B.C., several jury courts were created by the so called ***leges iudiciorum publicorum***.[106] Such statutes laid down for a significant part of crimes the following issues:[107]
Firstly, a legal description of the offences concerned.
Secondly, a legally ordered punishment.
Thirdly, a legally required and regulated trial by jury court.
Here, under the dictatorship of *Sulla* (82–79 B.C.) seven of those courts called *quaestiones* were established for specific crimes, namely inter alia the following ones:[108]

- Murder, in addition poisoning and harmful black magic both equated with murder.[109]
- *Sacrilegium* and *peculatus* (apparently meaning: theft from a temple; peculation, theft or fraudulent acts against public property or public assets).[110]
- *Falsum* (here meaning counterfeiting of testaments and coins).[111]

---

99 See text above, III 1.
100 Thereto: v. Hippel (supra note 56), p. 59, 62; Krey, Interrogational Torture, Volume I, p. 26 at the end, 27, 28; Wesel (supra note 1), side note 133.
101 Meaning power of life and death (see text above, IV 1 a (1) with footnote 85).
102 v. Hippel, p. 59, 61 et seq.; Krey (supra note 100), p. 26–28; Wesel, side note 133.
103 v. Hippel, p. 62 footnote 2, p. 65 footnote 4; Krey, p. 28 with footnote 52, 54.
104 Der Kleine Pauly, Lexikon der Antike (supra note 52), keyword Tresviri, 1 b; Wesel, side note 133; also see Krey, p. 28 with footnote 53.
105 Der Kleine Pauly, keyword Tresviri, 1 b; Wesel, side note 133; also see Krey, page 28 with footnote 53.
106 Thereto: v. Hippel, p. 62 at the end up to p. 65; Der Kleine Pauly, Vol. 4, keyword "Quaestio"; Krey, Interrogational Torture, Volume I (supra note 6), p. 28; Krey, About Magicians and Witches (supra note 6), p. 241; Krey, Keine Strafe ohne Gesetz (supra note 28), side note 35 with further references; Mommsen (supra note 84), p. 186 et seq., 203 and more often; Wesel (supra note 1), side note 133.
107 See supra note 106.
108 Thereto: v. Hippel (supra note 56), p. 64; Mommsen, p. 203 and more; Wesel, side note 133.
109 See with further references: v. Hippel, p. 64 footnote 5; Krey, About Magicians and Witches (supra note 6), p. 241 with footnote 43.
110 v. Hippel, p. 64 with footnote 4; Mommsen, p. 760 et seq., 764 with footnote 2; Wesel, side note 133.
111 v. Hippel, p. 64 with footnote 7; Mommsen, p. 669; Wesel, side note 133.

- *Iniuria atrox* (meaning serious assaults on third parties).[112]

As punishment for such crimes usually the banishment of the offender concerned was imposed, even though exceptionally death penalty could be applied.[113]

e) leges iudiciorum publicorum: no Enactment of the Principle "nulla poena sine lege". 23
The mentioned *leges iudiciorum publicorum* meant nothing less than a significant step towards the rule of statute law in criminal matters, namely not only in the field of substantive criminal law but also to some extent for criminal proceedings. Nevertheless, it would be anachronistic to state that

> the well-known principle **"nulla poena sine lege"** (no punishment without statute law) in Rome already applied during the last two centuries B.C.

Such a statement would be incorrect for the following reasons:
(1) The *leges iudiciorum publicorum* did not cover the majority of the then existing types of crimes.
(2) The present-day continental European criminal law is ruled by the principle *nulla poena sine lege.*[114] With regard to legal regulations **establishing or aggravating punishment** this principle lays down four prohibitions.[115]

> For a better understanding of those prohibitions you will find below the classical formulation of such principle laid down in Art. 103 paragraph 2 of the German Federal Constitution (called *Grundgesetz, GG*), saying:
> *Eine Tat kann nur bestraft werden, wenn die Strafbarkeit gesetzlich bestimmt war, bevor die Tat begangen wurde.*
> Near translation: An act may be punished only if it was defined by statute law as a criminal offence before the act was committed.

The four prohibitions, mentioned above, are the following:
Firstly, the prohibition of **retroactive effect** *(ex post facto law)*
That ban of legal regulations establishing (or aggravating) punishment with retroactivity[116] applied only to a limited extent during the time of the late Roman republic. This is because of the fact that the retroactivity of criminal laws then was not seen as problematic **under the following condition:**[117]
The criminal provision in question only covered such misdeeds to be characterized as serious crimes worthy of punishment even without a respective criminal statute.

> Here, one could talk of "*natürliche Verbrechen*" (meaning serious crimes by their very nature).[118]

---

112 v. Hippel, p. 64 with footnote 6; Mommsen, p. 789 et seq.; Wesel, side note 133.

113 v. Hippel, p. 62 footnote 6; Mommsen, p. 220, 941, 942; Wesel, side note 133. – Already see text above, IV. 1. a), (3) with footnote 96. –

114 Thereto with lots of references: Krey, Keine Strafe ohne Gesetz (supra note 28), side notes 1 to 137; Krey, Deutsches Strafrecht, Allgemeiner Teil, Lehrbuch in Deutsch und Englisch, Teil I: Grundlagen – German Criminal Law, General Part, Textbook in German and English, Volume I: Basics (Publishing Company W. Kohlhammer, Stuttgart), 2002, side notes 44–114; Krey/Esser, Deutsches Strafrecht, Allgemeiner Teil, 6th edition (Publishing Company W. Kohlhammer, Stuttgart), 2016, side note 38–107.

115 The following remarks refer to the German Law, insofar being exemplary. Thereto supra note 114.

116 Thereto elaborated, in detail and with further references: Krey, Keine Strafe ohne Gesetz, side note 1, 48 et seq.; Krey, Deutsches Strafrecht, Allgemeiner Teil – German Criminal Law, General Part (supra note 114), side note 44, 55–58, 59 et seq,; Krey/Esser (supra note 114), side note 38 et seq., 49, 52–77.

117 With regards to the following see with further references: Schöckel, Die Entwicklung des strafrechtlichen Rückwirkungsverbots bis zur französischen Revolution, 1968, p. 6–10; Schreiber, Gesetz und Richter, Zur geschichtlichen Entwicklung des Satzes nullum crimen, nulla poena sine lege, 1976, p. 17, 22; also see Krey, Keine Strafe ohne Gesetz, side note 48; each oft them with reference to Cicero (In Verrem).

118 See Krey (supra note 117), side note 48, additionally 51, 52 and more often.

In contrast, where a criminal provision was concerned, covering such acts which had not been punishable before the enactment of that statute and whose worthiness of punishment was not self-evident, a prohibition of retroactivity was deemed necessary.
Secondly, the prohibition of **customary law**[119] establishing or aggravating punishment
During the Roman Republic there was no such ban. So, customary law and judge-made law (case law) could serve as a source for punishment. Furthermore, the mentioned criminal law provisions laid down by the Law of the Twelve Tables and later on by the *leges iudiciorum publicorum* did not contain an exhaustive regulation (in German: *abschließende Regelung*)[120] and thus left room for customary law. In the end, during the period between the Twelve Tables and the *leges iudiciorum publicorum* no comprehensive criminal legislation occurred; additionally, in the time between the latter statutes and the end of the era of the Roman Republic (27 B.C. with the Principate of *Augustus*) the criminal legislation was resting to a great extent.
Thirdly, prohibition of **analogy** establishing or aggravating punishment
Upon a more precise analysis, this ban of analogy establishes a restriction for any **application** of statutory criminal law provisions, which is not covered by the statute's wording.
Hence, this wording as a formal restriction constitutes a limit on any legal interpretation of statutory law establishing or aggravating punishment.[121] However, such prohibition of analogy

– and more generally the principle *nulla poena sine lege* itself –

was foreign to the Roman Law.[122] Here, the legal interpretation was not limited by the respective criminal provision's wording.
Fourthly prohibition of too uncertain criminal statutes (principle of certainty)
Criminal statutes ought to be sufficiently precise. This is true for both, the statutory definition of the criminal offence at hand and the statutory range of punishment.[123] Such ban as well was foreign to Roman Criminal Law.[124] Numerous of its criminal provisions were characterized by a significant lack of certainty; this imperfection of criminal provisions is quite typical for Roman Criminal Law. The following examples may illustrate this statement:
The "*crimen iniuria*" covered, inter alia, bodily injury, defamation, trespass and disregard for the rights of a Roman Citizen.[125]

---

119 Thereto elaborated, in detail and with further references: Krey, Keine Strafe ohne Gesetz, side note 1, 35.; Krey, Deutsches Strafrecht, Allgemeiner Teil – German Criminal Law, General Part (supra note 114), side note 106 et seq,; Krey/Esser (supra note 114), side note 49, 98 et seq.

120 v. Hippel (supra note 56), p. 62 et seq., 67; Krey, Keine Strafe ohne Gesetz, side note 35; Mommsen (supra note 84), p.127–131.

121 Thereto elaborated, in detail and with further references: Krey, Studien zum Gesetzesvorbehalt im Strafrecht. Eine Einführung in die Problematik des Analogieverbots, 1977, p. 19–248; Krey, Keine Strafe ohne Gesetz, side note 1, 70 et seq.; Krey, Deutsches Strafrecht, Allgemeiner Teil – German Criminal Law, General Part (supra note 114), side note 85 et seq,; Krey/Esser (supra note 114), side note 49, 78 et seq.

122 v. Hippel, p. 54 et seq., p. 65 footnote 1, p. 77; v. Hippel, Deutsches Strafrecht, Volume II, 1930 (reprint 1971), p. 33; Krey, Keine Strafe ohne Gesetz, side note 35, 70; Mommsen, p.127; Schreiber (supra note 117), p. 17 ff, 25; Wacke, Juristische Schulung (JuS, i.e. a German Law Journal), 1980, 204 et seq. with further references.

123 Bundesverfassungsgericht (BVerfG i.e. Federal Constitutional Court) in BVerfG E (decisions of the BVerfG – official reports of cases –), 25, 269, 285.

124 v. Hippel, Volume I (supra note 56), p. 54 et seq., 77; Krey, Keine Strafe ohne Gesetz, side note 84; v. Liszt/Schmidt, Lehrbuch des Deutschen Strafrecht, 25th edition, 1927, p. 41.

125 See inter alia: v. Hippel, Volume I, p. S. 64 footnote 6 (iniuria atrox, i.e. serious iniuria); v. Liszt/ Schmidt, Lehrbuch des Deutschen Strafrechts, 25. edition 1927, p. 257; Mommsen (supra note 84), p. 785, 787, 790 et seq.; Wesel (supra note 1) side note 133.

The *"crimen vis"* (i.e. illegal use of force) covered an indefinite number of cases, where force is used or imminent, such as[126]

- rioting in the streets, disturbing the public peace committed by gangs;[127]
- carrying weapons on public streets or places;[128]
- violent damage to property;[129]
- violent deprivation of liberty;[130]
- rape;[131]
- abuse of power.[132]

f) **Conclusion.** Anyhow, one may say: During the period of the Roman Republic there were some significant developments towards the rule of law in criminal proceedings. Furthermore, due to the then dominating **idea of man**, regarding the Roman Citizens,[133] their life and limb in principle were untouchable; this image and self-perception of Roman Freemen in particular resulted in the following **basic principles** of the Roman Criminal Law at that time: 24

Death penalty was unusual and undesirable. Moreover, where exceptionally perpetrators had to face the imposition and execution of such punishment, in principle they could evade this penalty by going into banishment.

In addition, bodily mutilation and whipping against Roman Citizens as well were undesirable; so, in the last centuries of the Roman Republic those penalties were abolished.[134]

However, the **dark sides** of the Roman Criminal Law in times of the Republic should not be ignored; here, in particular the following shall be pointed out:

(1) The class justice against slaves and members of the lower class in criminal cases by the *tresviri capitales.*[135]

(2) The *coercitio* (penal/disciplinary power) of Roman Consuls and Praetors, even though such power was limited by the right of appeal to the people *(provocatio ad populum)* in case of capital punishment[136] and, during the second and first century B.C., by the prohibition of corporal punishment against Roman Citizens.[137]

(3) And last but not least, the dark time of the Roman Civil Wars between 133 up to 30 B.C.,[138] when all legal protections mentioned above against killing Roman Citizens were violated by arbitrary actions and bloodthirsty massacres against the respective losers

– in line with the brutal motto *"vae victis"* (Latin, meaning: woe to the defeated).

---

126 As regards the following see elaborated, in detail and with further references Mommsen, p. 655 et seq.

127 Mommsen, p. 655, 657, 662; Wesel, side note 133.

128 Mommsen, p. 657, 658.

129 Mommsen, p. 660, 661.

130 Mommsen, p. 664.

131 Mommsen, p. 664, 665.

132 Mommsen, p. 663, 664.

133 S text above IV, 1, a (4) with footnotes 98, 99.

134 v. *Hippel*, Volume I (supra note 56), p. 62 (at the end) up to 65; *Krey*, Interrogational Torture, Volume I (supra note 6), p. 28; *Mommsen* (supra note 84), p. 922, 923, 941 et seq., 981 et seq.; *Wesel* (supra note 1), side note 133. Also see text above, IV 1 a (4), b.

135 See text above, IV 1 c, with footnote 105.

136 Already see text above, IV 1 b with footnote 102.

137 See supra note 134.

138 Already see Krey, p. 28. More detailed Greg Woolf, Rom, Die Biographie eines Weltreichs, Deutsche Ausgabe (translated into German by Andreas Wittenburg) J. G. Cotta, 2015, 2017, p. 148 et seq., 150, 151, 160 (Tiberius and Gaius Gracchus), 155, 174, 177 et seq., 194 (Marius and Sulla), 175, 181 et seq., 184, 192 et seq., 194 (Pompeius and Caesar), 160, 192 et seq. (Octavian and Marc Antony); original English edition: Rome. An Empire's Story, by Greg Woolf, 2012.

2. Roman Imperial Era

25 This era started with *Augustus's* Principate (27 B.C. to 14 A.D.). The Western Roman Empire ended 476 A.D. with the deposition of the emperor *Romulus Augustus.*
a) Already during the **classic era** of the Principate (1st and 2nd century A.D.) the Roman Criminal Law's character increasingly changed in the direction of severity and cruelty.[139] This is true for both substantive criminal law and criminal procedure law. The mentioned jury trials pursuant to the *leges iudiciorum publicorum*[140] gradually were replaced by imperial tribunals where imperial officials held office.[141]
Death penalty gradually was threatened and executed more frequently. Corporal punishment as well became more and more accepted against members of the lower class as supplementary penalty in case of forced labour conviction (particularly sentencing to forced mining labour).[142]
Furthermore, the Roman Princeps *ab initio* was considered as carrier of the state authority, more precisely with unlimited power saying: *princeps legibus solutus* (i.e. the emperor is not bound by the law).[143]

However, this statement does not exactly apply to the aforesaid classic era of the Principate. Rather, such unlimited power was absolutely prevailing not until the subsequent post-classical period of the Roman Empire.

b) During that **post-classical period** (since the 3rd century A.D.), the tendency towards a more severe and cruel criminal law with **death penalty, whipping/flagellation**, brutal **forced labour** and finally

– since the time of the Roman emperor *Diocletian* (284 to 311 A.D.)[144] –

mutilation as a criminal punishment was rising. This development primarily affected the *humiliores* (members of the lower class).[145]
As regards the **death penalty** against Roman Citizens, in addition to the common way of its **execution** by beheading with the sword[146] step by step more cruel means of its execution became habitual, such as crucifixion and death by burning.[147]
However, in principle capital punishment and its execution against members of the upper classes (*honestiores*, particularly Roman Senators and Roman Knights) still was unwanted, apart from crimes like *crimen laesae maiestatis* (crime against the emperor).[148]
c) The serious deterioration in the situation of substantive criminal law since the days of the Roman Imperial Era unfortunately was supplemented by an undesirable development in the field of criminal procedure law, namely the increasing evolution of interrogational torture into an admissible instrument of taking evidence:
In times of the Roman Republic, interrogational torture was allowed only against slaves, but not against Roman Citizens.[149] Since the Principate of *Tiberius*, successor of *Augustus*, torturing even Roman Citizens more and more was admitted; however

---

139 Krey, p. 30; Wesel, side note 133.
140 See text above, IV 1 d).
141 v. Hippel, p.65; Wesel, side note 133.
142 v. Hippel, p. 69 with further references; Mommsen, p. 949 et seq.
143 Ulpian, Digesten (D. 1, 3, 31); v. Hippel (supra note 56), p. 66 et seq.
144 v. Hippel, p. 69; Mommsen (supra note 84), p. 982, 983.
145 v. Hippel, p. 68 with footnote 6, 69; Krey, Interrogational Torture, Volume I (supra note 6), p. 30.
146 Initially beheading with the axe. Thereto in detail Mommsen, p. 917, 918, 923 et seq.
147 Regarding the forms of death penalty and their execution see in detail and with further references Mommsen, p. 911 up to p. 944.
148 v. Hippel, p. 68 with footnote 6, p. 70 with footnote 6; Mommsen, p. 942, 943.
149 Thereto with further references Krey, p. 26, 29, 30, 32.

in principle only against *humiliores*, whereas members of the upper classes *(honestiores)*, in addition soldiers, in principle were excluded from torture.[150]

3. Outlook

The Roman Criminal Law of the **Imperial Era** was 26

– since its start but strengthened during its post-classical period[151] –

characterized by an increasingly widespread use of **death penalty** and brutal corporal punishment up to mutilation, in addition by the aforesaid use of interrogational torture.

About one thousand years later, this undesirable development might have been one of the contributory causes for the then occurring **terrible decline** of criminal law, namely through the ***Peinliches Strafrecht***, characterized by cruel punishment striking life and limb, in conjunction with the ***Inquisitionsprozess,*** carried out *ex officio* and increasingly dominated by interrogational **torture**[152]. In Germany, such decline took place during the Late Middle Ages and the first two centuries of the Early Modern Age (the 16th and 17th one), more precisely:

Since the 13th century, the beginning of the Late Middle Ages, the floodgates to capital punishment and interrogational torture in criminal proceedings were opened.[153] However, the triumph of the *Peinliche Strafrecht* as well as of the *Inquisitionsprozess* with its reign of terror by using interrogational torture took place not until the 16th and 17th century.[154]

The author's assumption expressed above, that there was a contributory causation of the Roman Imperial Era's Law for *Peinliches Strafrecht* and *Inquisitionsprozess* is based on the **Reception of the Roman Law**[155], which began in the High Middle Ages. Yet, how important the influence of such Reception was, may be left open here.

---

150 See Krey, p. 31, 32, 33.

151 See text above, 2. a, b.

152 Thereto in detail and with numerous references: Krey, Interrogational Torture in Criminal Proceedings – Reflections on Legal History –, Vol. II, in: Rechtspolitisches Forum (Legal Policy Forum), Institut für Rechtspolitik (IRP), University of Trier. No 73, 2015, p. 14 et seq., 24 et seq.; Krey, About Magicians and Witches (supra note 6), p. 250, 251.

153 See: Krey, Interrogational Torture, Vol. II (supra note 152), p. 14–23; Krey, About Magicians and Witches (supra note 6), p. 250, 251.

154 Krey, Interrogational Torture, Vol II, p. 14, 24 et seq., 30 et seq.; Krey, About Magicians and Witches, p. 251.

155 See text above, IV, with footnote 78–81. Already see Krey, Interrogational Torture Vol. I (supra note 6) p. 43.

Chapter Three: **The Early Middle Ages**

V. Beginning and End of this Era

The Western Roman Empire has ended 476 A.D.[156] Soon after, on its territory **the Kingdom of the Franks** arose.[157] This forming a new empire under the Frankish King *Chlodwig* (in English *Clovis*, 466–511 A.D.) at the same time is denoted as the **beginning** of the Middle Ages, here: the Early Middle Ages.[158] Hence, such beginning is generally dated on the end of the 5th century/early part of the 6th century.[159] **27**
The end of the Kingdom of the Francs, denoted by the **Kingdom's final partition** since the Treaty of Verdun (843 A.D.) under the sons of the 840 A.D. deceased Emperor *Louis the Pious*, at the same time indicated the **end** of the Early Middle Ages.[160]

These sons of *Louis*, all of them also being grandsons of *Charlemagne*, were

- *Lothar* (the oldest one);
- Charles the Bald;
- Louis the German.

By the Treaty of Verdun *Charles the Bald* got the western part of the Frankish Kingdom; *Louis the German* received the eastern part. The part in the middle between the western and the eastern one, called Middle Francia, was given to *Lothar* as *Lotharii Regnum*; this in conjunction with the imperial title as Emperor.[161]
However, that three-way split very soon became obsolete because *Lothar* died in 855 A.D. Subsequently the *Lotharii Regnum* (Middle Francia) was divided between *Charles the Bald* and *Louis the German*.[162]
The **definite** end of the Carolingian Empire is denoted by the election of *Conrad I* as King of East Francia in 911; more precisely: After the death of the last **Carolingian** King of East Francia, the Germanic tribes of this Kingdom elected *Conrad*, a Germanic Duke, as successor. By contrast, the Kingdom of West Francia at that time still was governed by the Carolingian Dynasty.[163]

---

156 Already see Krey, About Magicians and Witches. Reflections on Legal History. From the Ancient World up to the High Middle Ages, in: Festschrift for Lindacher, 2017, p. 243.
157 Wesel (supra note 1), side note 185 et seq. Already see Krey, Interrogational Torture in Criminal Proceedings. Reflections on Legal History, Vol. I, in: Rechtspolitisches Forum (Legal Policy Forum), Institut für Rechtspolitik (IRP), University of Trier, No 68, dated 2014, p. 34.
158 Fried, Das Mittelalter. Geschichte und Kultur, 2nd edition 2009, p. 8; Wesel, side note 185 et seq.; Winkler, Geschichte des Westens, 2009 (Jubiläumsedition, i.e. anniversary edition, 2013, p. 45).
159 Fried, p. 8; Gmür/Roth (supra note 51), side note 31; Wesel, side note 185.
160 See: Eisenhardt, Deutsche Rechtsgeschichte, 6th edition 2013, side note 3, 4–6; Fried, p. 86, 87 et seq., 91, 98 et seq., 100, 102, 103; Gmür/Roth, side note 31.
161 Eisenhardt, Deutsche Rechtsgeschichte, 6th edition 2013, side note 3, 4; Fried (supra note 78), p. 86 et seq., 96 et seq., 100, 102, 103; Wesel, side note 186.
162 Fried, p. 103.
163 Thereto: Eisenhardt, side note 4–6.
Anyhow, at the latest the election of the Saxon Duke Henry I in 919 as King of East Francia (today also called German King) denoted the very final end of the Frankish Empire.

VI. Extent and Importance of the Frankish Empire

28 In its period of glory under ***Charlemagne***, King since 768 A.D. and later on Emperor (coronation by the Pope in 800 A.D.),[164] the Kingdom of the Franks covered the whole Christian Western and Central Europe, apart from

- the British Isles;
- the Kingdom of Asturias/Galicia as Christian remains on the, at that time, Muslim Iberian Peninsula.[165]

There are a lot of merits, acquired by Frankish Kings, in establishing the requirements for a powerful empire being capable of development and of covering nearly the whole of Western and Central Europe. Here, primarily ***Charlemagne*** is to be named. In this context, the following areas being important for forming such a state should be mentioned:

Firstly, military and financial strength as well as an effective administration and legal order

As regards military and financial power, administration and legal order, the Frankish Kingdom under *Charlemagne* was, for those times, remarkably effective.[166] Here, the continuing influence of the Roman Law and tradition, particularly the Late Roman military law as well, should be noted.[167]

Secondly, the imprinting of culture and religion as well as of education and science by *Charlemagne* throughout Central Europe[168]

> Here, *Charlemagne's* successful efforts to improve the skills in Latin by replacing the widespread Vulgar Latin with the Classical Latin and, by doing so, to renew and expand the studies in Latin are to be emphasized. So, he created the basis for the enforcement of Latin as language of the church and of science.[169]

Thirdly, the close cooperation of the State with the church

Such cooperation already started under the Frankish King *Chlodwig*,[170] who had converted to Christianity in 496 A.D.,[171] and later culminated under ***Charlemagne.*** For his reign, the very close **link** between *imperium* and *sacerdotium* (meaning Empire and Roman Catholic Church) was characteristic.[172]

Regarding **death penalty**, this link had considerable effects for such sanction because the Church then had a negative approach towards blood feuds and capital punishment ("***ecclesia non sitit sanguinem***", meaning the Church has no thirst for blood).[173]

---

164 As regards this great Frankish King and later on (until his death in 814 A.D.) Emperor see the historical biographies by: Fried, Karl der Große, 2013; Weinfurter, Karl der Große. Der heilige Barbar, 2013.

165 Fried, Das Mittelalter (supra note 78), p. 66; Weinfurter, in front of p.1 and behind p. 352; Wesel, side note 186.

166 Fried, Das Mittelalter, p. 58 et seq.

167 As to the military strength see inter alia: Fried, p. 28; in detail Weinfurter, p. 140, 141.

168 See Fried, Das Mittelalter, p. 66 et seq.

169 Fried, p. 66 et seq.

170 As regards this King see text above V, 1; concerning his cooperation with the Church see Wesel (supra note 1), side note 187.

171 Wesel, side note 187.

172 Fried, Das Mittelalter (supra note 78), p. 63; Wesel, side note 186.

173 v. Hippel, Deutsches Strafrecht, Band 1, 1925 (reprint 1971), p. 83 with footnote 4, p. 90; however, regarding the reign of the Carolingian dynasty more restrictive on p. 113. Already see: Krey in Festschrift for Lindacher (supra note 6), p.249; Krey, Interrogational Torture in Criminal Proceedings – Reflections on Legal History – Vol. II, in: Rechtspolitisches Forum (Legal Policy Forum), Institut für Rechtspolitik (IRP), University of Trier, No 73, dated 2015, p. 17; Krey, About Magicians and Witches, Reflections on Legal History. The Late Middle Ages: Opening the Floodgates to Cruel Witch Hunting by Use of Torture and Capital Punishment. In: Festschrift for Manuel da Costa Andrade, University of Coimbra, Vol. II, in 2017, p. 423, 426 with footnote 10.

Therefore, the Church used some good instruments to prevent blood feuds on the one hand and sentencing to death or at least its execution on the other hand:
In case of "*Sühneverträge*"

(i.e. expiation contracts, meaning an agreement between the offender's clan and the victim's one, aiming at replacing clan feuds by providing **blood money**[174]),

the Church often took over the blood money's payment if the perpetrator and his clan were unable to pay.[175]
In case of death sentencing (respectively threatened sentence to death) by the state, the church often asserts its significant influence to save the perpetrator's life by replacing the death penalty or at least its execution with the perpetrator's **banishment.**
Fourthly, saving the heritage of the Roman antiquity
Charlemagne laid the foundation for such saving, namely by the mentioned renewal of the Classical Latin and through the extensive preservation of ancient sources written down on **transient** papyrus by their copying on parchment, the latter being very expensive but **durable.**[176]
Finally, it should be noted that the **existence** of the powerful and aggressively expensive Kingdom of the Franks since *Charles Martell*, grandfather of *Charlemagne*, and in particular later on under *Charlemagne*, was of significant relevance for saving Middle and Western Europe from the Islamic Conquest.[177] In this context, the following keywords may be sufficient:

- The battle of Tours and Poitiers (732 A.D.) where the Frankish troops under *Charles Martell* and his allies defeated a great Muslim army which had invaded the south-west France[178] After the death of their military leader and the loss of many thousands of Muslim soldiers who died in battle and further many thousands of wounded Muslim fighters, the remnants of the Muslim army retreated to the Iberian Peninsula.
- The repeated and after all final expulsion of the Muslim conquerors out of the area around Narbonne (southern France) by the Frankish rulers during the 8th century A.D.[179]

VII. Legal Sources and Nature of the Frankish Law

1. Legal Sources

As regards this issue, the author can refer to some of his former publications.[180] **29**
The relevant insights and views stated there shall be reproduced here, but in an abbreviated version where possible and appropriate, however, partly in an extended version too. The same applies to the issues, discussed under the subsequent points **III 2** and **IV.**

a) In its core, the Law of the Kingdom of the Franks under *Charlemagne* was based on the so-called *leges barbarorum*, meaning tribal laws applying to the different Ger-

---

174 Thereto with further references Chapter Two, III 2 – regarding the Germanic Law – ; Krey, Interrogational Torture, Volume I (supra note 6), p. 20–22, 35–37; Krey, Festschrift for Lindacher (supra note 2), p. 238, 239.

175 Rüping/Jerouschek, Grundriss der Strafrechtsgeschichte, 6th edition 2011, side note 16; already see Krey, Interrogational Torture, Volume I (supra note 6), p. 36 at the end, 37.

176 In detail see Fried, Das Mittelalter, p. 67–69.

177 Abulafia, Das Mittelmeer, 2013, p. 333,334 et seq. (original English edition 2011, Penguin Books, The Great Sea …); Fried, Karl der Große (supra note 164), p. 43, 57, 60, 95 et the end.

178 Fried, Das Mittelalter (supra note 78), p. 48, 49; Weinfurter (supra note 164), p. 59.

179 Fried, Karl der Große (supra note 164), p. 43, 57, 60, 95 at the end, 612; Weinfurter, p. 59, 83.

180 Krey, Interrogational Torture (supra note 6), p. 34 et seq.; Krey, in: Festschrift for Lindacher, p. 243 et seq.

manic tribes who lived under the rule of the Frankish King. Here, the *Lex Salica* applying to the Franks as the reigning tribe and still being decisively influenced by traditional Germanic Law has to be pointed out.[181]
b) Additionally, there still was to a certain extent the influence of Roman Law, the latter being of relevant influence on the Roman inhabitants of the Kingdom as well as on the Christian Church.[182]
c) Finally, law of the King existed, in particular the capitularies of the Carolingian dynasty (King's edicts, in Latin: *Capitularia Regum Francorum*), most of them passed by *Charlemagne* and often covering criminal provisions. However, it is questionable how far such rules of the King were accepted and applied throughout the whole Empire of the Franks.[183]

2. The very Nature of the Frankish Law

30 As stated above, the law of the Frankish Kingdom in its core was based on the ***Leges Barbarorum*** being **Germanic Law**, even though written down in Latin by the Frankish Kings. Such Latin for a long time was "barbarically faulty"; however, since the end of the 8th century, those ***leges*** were carried out in a correct Latin version.[184] Because of the Germanic nature of the *Leges Barbarorum* and of their key importance for the Frankish Law it may be noted that Frankish Law essentially was Germanic Law.[185]
Hence, the Germanic idea of man (in German *"Menschenbild"*) outlined above[186] still remained predominant during the Age of the Frankish Kingdom, stating:
Life and limb of a Germanic freeman (in contrast to bondsmen and slaves) in principle were inviolable and therefore had to be respected by the general public.[187]
Accordingly, **mutilating penalties** and **bashing/whipping** against freemen being members of Germanic tribes who lived under the rule of Frankish Kings, for example
- Alemanni,
- Bavarians,
- Burgundians,
- Frisians,
- Saxons,

were unwanted. **Death penalty** existed, however, in principle it was a foreign matter.[188]

---

181 As regards the Lex Salica see: Gmür/Roth (supra note 51), side note 32–35, 74; v. Hippel (supra note 56), p. 109, 111, 113; Rüping/Jerouschek (supra note 51), side note 8, 16; Weinfurter (supra note 164), p. 33; Wesel (supra note 1), side note 178, 191 et seq.

182 Krey, Interrogational Torture (supra note 6), p. 34; Rüping/Jerouschek, side note 13, 17; Wesel, side note 191, 201.

183 v. Hippel (supra note 56), p. 111 with footnote 3; Rüping/Jerouschek, side note 17; Weinfurter, p. 33; Wesel (supra note 1), side note 191. Thus, Wesel rightly stated that the importance of those Capitularia were clearly overestimated. Additionally see text below, IV, 2.

184 Gmür/Roth, side note 35.

185 Krey: Festschrift for Lindacher (supra note 6), p. 243, 244; Krey, Interrogational Torture, Vol I (supra note 6), p. 34, 35.

186 See text above Chapter Two, III, 1; already see: Krey, Festschrift for Lindacher, p. 237, 238; Krey, Interrogational Torture (supra note 6), p. 19, 20.

187 As regards the old Germanic Law see supra note 186; concerning the **Frankish Law** see inter alia: Krey, Festschrift for Lindacher, p. 244; Krey, Interrogational Torture (supra note 6), p. 35, 36, 37 at the end, 38.

188 Krey, Festschrift for Lindacher, p. 244 (at the end), 245; Krey, Interrogational Torture, p. 37, 38. – Thereto **in detail** text below, IV.

VIII. About the Criminal Law of the Frankish Kingdom

1. Frankish Criminal Law in its core being Private Criminal Law

Due to the above mentioned nature of the Frankish Law as in its core Germanic Law, the criminal law applying to the aforesaid (and other) Germanic tribes, living under the rule of Frankish Kings, in principle still was **Private Criminal Law** – in accordance with the old Germanic Tradition.[189] Thus, **"external offences"** committed by members of one clan against members of another clan were purely private affairs; this even held in cases of capital crimes.[190] 31

a) In principle, such external crimes resulted in clan feuds, or in **"expiation contracts"** (in German: *Sühneverträge*) aiming at replacing clan feuds by providing **blood money**: On the basis of a contract between the offender's clan and the victim's one, the latter could waive the right to blood feud in return for blood money

– offered as an attempt to satisfy the desire for revenge of the victim's clan –.[191]

b) Clan feuds, characterized by mutual bloodshed within an almost endless cycle of retaliatory revenge between the clans involved, typically were highly undesirable for the public authority and at the same time for the Church.[192] So, expiation contracts were in the very interest of the King and the Church, both aiming at the prevention of bloodshed.

c) This insight is particularly clarified by the fact that the mentioned *Leges Barbarorum* largely were nothing more than **catalogues of blood money**, e.g. Wergild in case of manslaughter: Such *leges* ordered the Wergild's amount (respectively the comparable material compensation in case of other serious crimes) to be paid in order to replace clan feuds with expiation contracts.[193] Here, a severe differentiation between the victims concerned according to their tribal affiliation, other class distinctions, and their gender, etc. is to be ascertained.

Such a difference, for example, was made between killing (or injuring):

- members of the Frankish tribe as the ruling one;
- members of other Germanic tribes, living under the rule of Frankish Kings;
- Roman inhabitants of the Frankish Kingdom;
- priests and
- women.

Here, the respective amount of the Wergild in case of killing such kind of victims is fixed inter alia by the *Lex Ribvaria* (one of the aforesaid *Leges Barbarorum*) as follows:

- 200 shillings for killing a Frank;
- 160 shillings for killing a member of another Germanic tribe;
- 100 shillings for killing a Roman inhabitant;
- 600 shillings for killing a freeborn priest;
- 700 shillings for killing a pregnant woman together with her foetus.[194]

---

189 See text above Chapter Two, III 2. Already see: Krey, Festschrift for Lindacher (supra note 6), p. 238 et seq.; Krey, Interrogational Torture, Vol. I (supra note 6), p. 19–22; both with further references.

190 Fried, Das Mittelalter (supra note 78), p. 40; Gmür/Roth (supra note 51), side note 35, 62, 74; v. Hippel (supra note 56), p. 109–113; Rüping/Jerouschek (supra note 51), side note 8–11; Wesel (supra note 1), side note 178, 191 et seq., side note 199.

191 Already see text above Chapter Two, III, 2 b, c with further references; Krey, Interrogational Torture, Vol. I, p. 20, 21.

192 Fried, Das Mittelalter, p. 41; v. Hippel, p. 110, 111, 113.

193 Gmür/Roth, side note 74; v. Hippel, p. 109, 111; Rüping/Jerouschek, side note 8; Wesel, side note 178, 191 et seq.

194 As regards the text above see in detail: Kroeschell, Deutsche Rechtsgeschichte Bd. 1, 13th edition, 2008, 43 et seq; Rüping/Jerouschek (supra note 51), side note 10, 11. Also see Wesel, side note 199.

The latter rule might has been based less on a high appreciation for women in general, but on the importance of pregnant women for the continued existence of any tribe.

d) The state authority's influence on the replacement of clan feuds with the mentioned *"Sühneverträge"* (i.e. expiation contracts) was rising.[195] Thereby, beside the blood money to be paid to the victim's clan, in addition a *fredus* (peace money) must be paid to the public authority if the latter was involved in the respective contract negotiations, in typical represented by a judge.[196]

Ultimately, in case of external offences[197] Carolingian Kings tried to enforce the clans of the victims and of the offenders to enter into *"Sühneverträge"* (expiation contracts) instead of carrying out clan feuds as blood feuds. However, in the end such attempts were in vain.[198]

e) The firm rejection of blood revenge and clan feuds by the Church as mentioned above often resulted in **church support** for the payment of the respective blood money, as far as the clan concerned was unable to pay.[199]

2. Elements of Public Criminal Law within the Law of the Frankish Kingdom

32 Summing up, criminal law in its core still was Private Criminal Law. Nevertheless, there also was to some extent **Public Criminal Law:**

a) The so called *"Königsbann"* of the Frankish Kings as their power to **ban certain serious misdeeds** (such as treason, deserting in the battle, and high treason) **under threat of punishment** was not laid down in the *Leges Barbarorum*. However, at least for a narrow range of application, such power might have been accepted at any case under Carolingians rule, quasi as customary law.

b) Accordingly, the mentioned **capitularies** of the Carolingian dynasty (King's edicts, in Latin: *Capitularia Regum Francorum*),[200] carried out as law of the King in the form of **written law,** often covered rules on criminal matters. Most of such penal provisions of the King were laid down by *Charlemagne*.

Subject of such capitularies particularly were crimes against the King and/or his royal power (in Latin: *crimen laesae maiestatis*), in addition also other serious offences against the general public like treason or deserting in the battle.[201]

Here, penalties striking life and limb (in German: *peinliche Strafen*) by the authority were provided.[202] However, death penalty or at least its execution often was replaced with

- banishment/ostracising, or
- expiation payment (in German: *Sühnegeld*), or

---

195 In particular under Charlemagne; see Fried (supra note 78), p. 41.

196 Gmür/Roth (supra note 51), side note 24, 62, 74; v. Hippel (supra note 56), p. 111 with; Eb. Schmidt, Einführung in die Geschichte der deutschen Strafrechtspflege, 3rd edition 1965, p. 25.

197 See text above, Chapter One, IV, 1.

198 Fried, Das Mittelalter, p. 41, 85, 86; v. Hippel, p. 111 with footnote 2; Eb. Schmidt, p. 24.

199 See text above, Chapter One, II, 2, Thirdly (with footnote 21).

200 As regards the requirement of the **consent of the Frankish Kingdom's high nobility and bishops** see: Gmür/Roth (supra note 51), side note 36, 78; Wesel (supra note 1), side note 194.

201 As regards the text above see: Fried, p. 40; v. Hippel, p. 112 et seq.; Krey, Interrogational Torture Vol. I (supra note 6), p. 37; Rüping/Jerouschek (supra note 51), side note 13, 14; Weinfurter (supra note 164), p. 138, 139.

202 Fried, p. 40; Gmür/Roth, side note 78; v. Hippel, p. 112 et seq.; Wesel, side note 199.

– imprisonment (via equity), for example as custody in a monastery[203]

Anyhow, as already mentioned, it is questionable how far such rules of the King were accepted and applied throughout the whole Empire of the Franks.[204]

3. Implications for the Nature of the Early Middle Ages

The findings mentioned above may allow the following statement: From a criminal law standpoint, the Early Middle Ages was no part of the so-called **dark** Middle Ages, mostly called **Dark Ages.**[205] This value judgement particularly is also true from the standpoint of General History; such insight has been emphasized in detail and convincingly by *Fried* to whom reference is made here.[206] Finally, such assessment is confirmed by the fact that the Early Middle Ages was not blemished by **bloody persecution** of witches/sorcerers to a relevant extent, neither carried out nor tolerated by the Church or the King[207] – but this is another issue. **33**

203 As to the text above see: v. Hippel (supra note 56), p. 112–113 at the end; Krey in Festschrift for Lindacher (supra note 6), p. 243–245; Krey (supra note 201), p. 37, 38 with footnote 82; Rüping/Jerouschek, side note 20.
As to the replacement of death penalty with life-long custody in monasteries see: Fried, Karl der Große (supra note 164), p. 185–189; Weinfurter, p. 92–95; both referring to the elimination of **Duke Tassilo III by Charlemagne.**

204 See text above III, 1 c with further references.

205 Krey in Festschrift for Lindacher, p. 243, 244. Already see text above, III 2, IV 1, 2 b.

206 Fried, Das Mittelalter (supra note 78), p. 7, 8, 536 et seq. with p. 35 et seq., 58 et seq.

207 Thereto in detail Krey in Festschrift for Lindacher (supra note 6), p. 243 to 247.

Chapter Four: **The High Middle Ages**

IX. The Beginning and End of the High Middle Ages. Delimitation between this Era and the Late Middle Ages as well as the Early Modern Age

1. The Beginning of the High Middle Ages

The end of the Kingdom of the Franks as ending of the Early Middle Ages (usually dated end of the 9th century A.D./beginning of the 10th)[208] at the same time denotes the **beginning of the era of the High Middle Ages.**[209] Concurrently, there was the beginning of the German Empire under King *Conrad I* (911–918) and in particular King *Henry I* (Duke of Saxony), King of the German Empire 919–936. So, with a certain degree of simplification, it can be said: The era of the High Middle Ages started at the beginning of the 10th century. **34**

2. The End of the High Middle Ages: An Overview of this Problem

In contrast, the **end** of the High Middle Ages, and at the same time the beginning of the Late Middle Ages, is much more controversial: **35**
a) On the one hand, nowadays some relevant statements in the literature on legal history forego the differentiation between High Middle Ages and Late Middle Ages when discussing the period from the end of the Early Middle Ages up to the beginning of the Early Modern Age (approximately 1500 A.D.).[210]
b) On the other hand, recently even the distinction between the Middle Ages and the Early Modern Age (circa 1500–1800), more precisely the latter's first two centuries, is questioned pursuant to the nature of things.[211]
As regards this standpoint, the following arguments are named:
Firstly, the usual differentiation between the Dark Ages (in German: finsteres Mittelalter) and the first two centuries of the Early Modern Age, starting about 1500 and ending 1700, was incorrect pursuant to the nature of things. This was because much more important than events such as the **discovery of America** ("The New World"), and **Martin Luther's Reformation** together with the Augsburg religious peace[212], (and other highlights of the 16th century) was the **heyday of the Middle Ages** during the 12th century, namely the nowadays often so-called "kleine Renaissance" (meaning an early Renaissance). **Here the European Modern Time had started.**[213]
To clarify this starting, the following keywords may be sufficient:

---

208 See text above, Chapter One, I 2.

209 Gmür/Roth (supra note 51), side note 86 et seq.; already see: Krey, Interrogational Torture Vol. I (supra note 6), p. 41; Krey in Festschrift for Lindacher (supra note 6), p. 247; Schneidmüller/Weinfurter, Die deutschen Herrscher des Mittelalters, 2003, p. 12, 15 et seq.

210 Fried, Das Mittelalter (supra note 78), p. 7, 8, 98 et seq., 165 et seq., 186 et seq., 257 et seq., 289 et seq.; Rüping/Jerouschek (supra note 51), side note 26–84, 85 et seq.; Wesel (supra note 1), side note 185, 202.

211 Fried, p. 7, 8, 536 et seq. (with 35 et seq., 58 et seq.); Krey, Interrogational Torture Vol. I (supra note 6), p. 41 et seq.; Krey, Interrogational Torture Vol. II (supra note 152), p. 14, 15 et seq., 23, 24 et seq., 25, 30, 36 et seq.; Krey in Festschrift for Lindacher, p. 247 et seq., 250, 251; Krey in Festschrift for Manuel da Costa Andrade Vol. II (supra note 173), p. 423, 425, 437 et seq.; Wesel, side note 185, 202.

212 The so-called Peace of Augsburg, dated 1555, aimed at ensuring religious freedom in Germany to a large extent; thereto: Gmür/Roth (supra note 51), side note 250, 261; Wesel, side note 241, 242.

213 Wesel, side note 185, 202

- The rise of cities becoming cultural and economic centers and enacting autonomous town statutes, in particular criminal ones;[214] here, the development of civil rights for free citizens has begun.
- The foundation of the first universities since the end of the 11th century (Bologna etc.), where Canon Law and in particular **Roman Law** pursuant to the rediscovered *Corpus Iuris Civilis* (published 533, 534) of the Byzantine Emperor *Justinian* was taught. Here, the so-called Reception of Roman Law started throughout Europe.[215]
- The just mentioned **Reception**, beginning during the High Middle Ages, namely in its last century, the 12th, and then becoming the predominant trend during the era of the Late Middle Ages (13th to 15th century).[216]

Secondly, there are statements in the literature on legal history saying:
From the criminal law's point of view, the first two centuries of the Early Modern Age (the 16th and 17th) by the very nature of the things were to be characterized as continuation of the Late middle Ages, or in parts even worse.[217]
To give reasons for this, the following statements may be sufficient:
Indeed, there may be some good **arguments**, which at first glance allow to characterize such centuries as Modern Age, particularly the mentioned below:[218]

- The so-called *Ewiger Landfrieden* (meaning Eternal Public Peace) in Germany, dated 1495, in connection with the establishment of two German Imperial High Courts, namely the *Reichskammergericht* (also in 1495) and shortly later the *Reichshofrat.*
- The Constitutio Criminalis Carolina, also called Peinliche Gerichtsordnung of the German Emperor Karl V, dated 1532.[219]
- The above mentioned discovery of America (1492) as well as *Martin Luther's* Reformation since 1517, and the Augsburg religious peace dated 1555.

However, there are **major reasons** for the differing view saying that the first two centuries of the Early Modern Age in its core were to be characterized as continuation of the Late Middle Ages. This applies for the following reasons:
(1) Unlike the High Middle Ages (10th to 12th century), the era of the **Late Middle Ages** (13th to 15th century) convincingly may be characterized as Dark Ages[220] because not until the latter era the floodgates were opened to such **awful aberration** of criminal law and criminal proceedings like the mentioned below:

- The gradual development of the so-called *"peinliches Strafrecht"* (meaning criminal law dominated by cruel punishment **striking life and limb**[221]).

---

214 Rüping/Jerouschek, side note 52 et seq.; Wesel, side note 202, 215, 216, 240.

215 Fried, Das Mittelalter (supra note 78), p. 110, 111, 195, 232 et seq., 359; v. Hippel (supra note 56), p. 90, 91, 159 et seq.; Rüping/Jerouschek (supra note 51), side note 29, 30–34; Wesel (supra note 1), side note 202, 215–217; already see Krey, Interrogational Torture Vol. I (supra note 6), p. 43.

216 See supra note 215; in addition, regarding the Late Middle Ages, Krey in Festschrift for Manuel da Costa Andrade, Vol II (supra note 173), p. 425 with footnote 4.

217 Already see Krey, Interrogational Torture Vol. II (supra note 152), p. 24, 25; Krey in Festschrift for Manuel da Costa Andrade, p. 437. Likewise: Fried, p. 535, 536 et seq.; Eb. Schmidt (supra note 60), p. 17, 18; similar; Gmür/Roth (supra note 51), side note 231; Wesel, side note 202, 241 et seq.

218 Already see Krey, Interrogational Torture Vol II, p. 24, 25 with further references.

219 For more details see: Krey, Keine Strafe ohne Gesetz. Einführung in die Dogmengeschichte des Satzes, „nullum crimen, nulla poena sine lege", 1983, side note 10, 11, 36, 50, 71, 85; Krey, Interrogational Torture Vol II, p. 25 to 30. **Source:** Schroeder (editor), Die Peinliche Gerichtsordnung Kaiser Karl V. mit Erläuterungen, 2000.

220 Krey, Interrogational Torture Vol II, p. 14, 15 et seq.; Krey in Festschrift for Lindacher (supra note 6), p. 250; Krey in Festschrift for Manuel da Costa Andrade, p. 442, 425 et seq.

221 The **death penalty** often was aggravated by cruel forms of execution such as burning to death, quartering or breaking on the wheel. **Corporal punishment** could even cover mutilation.

- The beginning of establishing the *"Inquisitionsprozess"*, carried out *ex officio* and ruled by brutal interrogational **torture.**
- The gradual development of merciless **witch hunting,** based on the model of the trials for **heresy** which due to the use of torture and death penalty by burning increasingly became cruel since the 13th century (being the beginning of the Late Middle Ages).[222]

(2) Hence, the floodgates were opened to the aforesaid awful aberration in the course of the Late Middle Ages. Consequently one can state: **The reign of terror** by *"Inquisitionsprozess"*, by *"Peinlichem Strafrecht"*, and in particular by horrible excesses of witch hunting with many tens of thousands victims in total may have its roots in the Late Middle Ages.[223]
However, such awful aberration of criminal law and criminal proceedings became predominant not until the Early Modern Age. Here, during the 16th and 17th century the monstrous waves of witch hunting occurred.[224] Both eras, the first two centuries of the Early Modern Age, and the Late Middle Ages, therefore are to be denoted as Dark Ages.[225]

3. The Author's Position on the Delimitation of the High Middle Ages

a) Anyhow, the publication at hand still will adhere to the traditional division of the era between the Kingdom of the Franks and the Modern Age in German historical scholarship, namely: High Middle Ages (10th-12th century), Late Middle Ages (13th-15th century) and Early Modern Age (16th-18th century). Accordingly, the **Middle Ages** covered about 1000 years: from the beginning of the Kingdom of the Franks as Early Middle Ages (around 500 A.D.) up to 1500 (start of the Early Modern Age). This division is traditional practice of German universities (*Fried*)[226], and it is not necessarily the task of Legal History, to change such tradition of the **general** science of history (*Wesel*).[227] So, despite the doubts mentioned above, the author still is orientated toward that traditional division – as already in earlier publications.[228] **36**
b) This orientation also applies specifically to the distinction between **High Middle Ages** and **Late Middle Ages,** if only because the following insight, already mentioned above:

> There was no significant development towards the rule of *"peinliches Strafrecht"*, *"Inquisitionsprozess"* with torture, and brutal witch hunting during the High Middle Ages, whereas such development started in the course of the Late Middle Ages and then got increasing importance during this era, as already noted in the text above, and will be explained in further detail below.

---

222 As to the text above, point (1), see: Fried (supra note 78), p. 278, 482, 483; Krey, Interrogational Torture Vol I (supra note 3), p. 44; Krey, Interrogational Torture Vol II, p. 14, 15–23; Krey in Festschrift for Lindacher, p.250, 251; Krey in Festschrift for Manuel da Costa Andrade, p. 437, 438; Wesel (supra note 1), side note 261.

223 Thereto in detail and with further references Krey, Festschrift for Manuel da Costa Andrade, p. 423 et seq.

224 Decker, Hexen. Magie, Mythen und die Wahrheit, 2004, p. 36 et seq., **45 et seq.**; Frenschkowski, Die Hexen. Eine kulturgeschichtliche Analyse, 2012, p. 23, 25, 120 et seq.; 127 et seq.; Gaskill, Hexen und Hexenverfolgung. Aus dem Englischen übersetzt von Blank-Sangmeister, 2013 (original English version Oxford 2013), p. 103–106; Gmür/Roth (supra note 51), side note 333; Rüping/Jerouschek (supra note 51), side note 145–148; Wesel, side note 261. Already see: Krey, Interrogational Torture Vol I, p. 44; Krey in Festschrift for Lindacher, p. 251; Krey Interrogational Torture Vol II, p. 25, 30–36; Krey in Festschrift for Manuel da Costa Andrade, p. 437.

225 Fried, p. 535; Krey in Festschrift for Lindacher, p. 250, 251; Krey in Festschrift for da Costa Andrade, p. 437.

226 Fried, p. 8. – Inter alia Gmür/Roth, side note 31, 86,136, 228, follow this praxis, too. -

227 Wesel, side note 185.

228 See inter alia the author's papers mentioned above (supra note 224).

X. General Assessment of the High Middle Ages

1. Continuing Predominance of Private Criminal Law

37 The end of the Kingdom of the Franks resulted in a standstill of the mentioned Royal tendencies towards the **development of public criminal law**, either by enacting King's edicts on criminal law or by trying to enforce the clans of the victims and of the offenders to enter into "Sühneverträge" (expiation contracts) instead of feuding.[229] Rather, **private criminal law** characterized by clan feuds and expiation contracts as methods of conflict resolution in case of crimes still was predominant during the first century of the High Middle Ages (10th), and in principle also in its second and third.[230]

2. The *"Gottesfrieden"* (Peace and Truce of God) and *"Landfrieden"* (Public Peace) as Instruments to restrict Feuds

38 Clan feuds (blood feuds) affected life and limb of the persons concerned, e.g. farmers being bondsmen, furthermore material assets like cattle and farmhouses. So, feuds disturbed the public peace significantly. Hence, the Church and the secular power of Emperors/Kings and Territorial Rulers such as Electors, Dukes, Landgraves, and Margraves, increasingly tried to limit the extent of feuds:
a) *"Gottesfrieden"* (in Latin: *Pax Dei*, *Treuga Dei*) carried out by Bishops were to be found since the 10th century, namely in southern France.[231] Step by step, they were supplemented by *"Landfrieden"*, enacted by the secular power during the next centuries in Germany, too.[232] Here, the most important ones of such "Landfrieden" were carried out by the German Emperor/King in agreement with the "Greats" among the German Territorial Rulers.[233]
b) Such *"Landfrieden"* aimed at significant restrictions of feuds. In order to ensure more public peace, the following limitations were carried out in most *"Landfrieden"*:
Firstly, the requirement to give formal notice before beginning a feud.[234]
Secondly, limitation of actions in relation to feuds such as attacks on people or objects. Here, certain categories of **persons** (e.g. priests, women, peasants), and of **objects** (churches, villages, mills, ploughs, and streets) shall enjoy immunity.[235]
Thirdly, permanently banning feuds at specific days, namely Thursday up to Sunday.[236]

---

229 Already see text above, Chapter Three, VIII 1 d.

230 Krey, Interrogational Torture Vol I (supra note 6), p. 41 at the end, 42 et seq.; Krey in Festschrift for Lindacher (supra note 6), p. 248, 249; Wesel (supra note 1), side note 236: since 1200 – the beginning of the Late Middle Ages – the public punishment had achieved the breakthrough.

231 Fried (supra note 78), p. 136; Rüping/Jerouschek (supra note 51), side note 48; Wesel, side note 207.

232 v. Hippel (supra note 56), p. 123; Krey, Interrogatioal Torture Vol I, p. 41, 42; Rüping/Jerouschek, side note 48, 49; Wesel, side note 207.

233 Gmür/Roth, side note 214; Rüping/Jerouschek, side note 50; Wesel, side note 207, 236. However, the most famous and important one of such Landfrieden, enacted by King and territorial princes – the "Mainzer Reichs-Landfrieden" dated 1235 – was no product of the High Middle Ages, because this era ended, as already mentioned, around 1200.

234 Gmür/Roth (supra note 51), side note 214; v. Hippel, p. 123.

235 Gmür/Roth, side note 214; v. Hippel, p. 123 with footnote 8; Rüping/Jerouschek, side note 49.

236 Fried (supra note 78), p. 136; Rüping/Jerouschek, side note 49.

XI. First Steps towards Public Criminal Law including Death Penalty

1. Threat of Punishment for Cases of breaking the Ban of Violence laid down in applicable *"Landfrieden"*

In this context, the importance of the mentioned *"Landfrieden"* for the issue **death penalty** lies in the fact that for cases of serious breaking the ban of violence a threat of severe punishment was laid down in the applicable *"Landfrieden"*: **39**
(1) In order to demonstrate the great importance, which the King and/or the respective German Territorial Rulers had attached to their agreements on enacting ***"Landfrieden"***, the latter rules generally covered penal provisions against cases of breaking the **bans laid down there.**[237] Such penal provisions carried out in *"Landfrieden"* even covered death penalty for breaking the public peace by violence.[238]
(2) Here, one root for the gradual development of public criminal law is to be seen, more precisely: This applies since the time of the 12th century,[239] the latest one of the **High Middle Ages.**
Nevertheless, during this era no opening the floodgates to a dominant *"peinliches Strafrecht"* striking life and limb as well as to the *"Inquisitionsprozess" ex officio* with brutal use of torture occurred. Rather, **by no means** there were significant waves of persecuting peace breakers pursuant to the rules of *"Landfrieden"*, and particularly there all the more was no significantly large number of death sentences and their execution in cases of such persecution.

2. Heresy Trials: Role Model for Public Criminal Law with Burning and Torturing not until the Late Middle Ages

As the author has already stated in previous papers, the heresy trials subsequently served as role model for brutal witch hunting.[240] However, not until the Late Middle Ages, heresy trials were shaped by the use of torture and sentencing to death by burning. As regards both, torture and capital punishment, even in the context of heresy trials these instruments still were undesirable even from the standpoint of the Church until the 13th century,[241] being the first one of the Late Middle Ages: **40**
During the High Middle Ages, the Church lived in accordance with the principle: *"ecclesia non sitit sanguinem"* (meaning the Church has no thirst for blood).[242] Not until the 13th century, the Church allowed and used **interrogational torture** and **death penalty by burning** in its fight against the rising Heretical Movements (Waldensians, and Cathars, and others); here, from the standpoint of the Church the question of power was concerned.[243]

3. The Rise of Cities with autonomous Town Statutes: No Development of Criminal Law striking Life and Limb associated with Torture during the High Middle Ages

As pointed out above,[244] in the course of the High Middle Ages, more precisely beginning at the end of the 11th century and then during the 12th, the rise of cities in **41**

---

237 Fried, p. 136; Rüping/Jerouschek, side note 48; Wesel (supra note 1), side note 207, 236; already see Krey, Interrogational Torture Vol I, p. 42 with further references.

238 Rüping/Jerouschek, side note 48; Wesel, side note 207, 236: death penalty for the "vredebreker" (old German, meaning peace-breaker).

239 Fried, p. 41; Wesel, side note 207, 236.

240 Krey, p. 16–18 with further references; Krey in Festschrift für Lindacher (supra note 6), p. 250.

241 Fried, p. 278; v. Hippel (supra note 56), p. 83 with footnote 4, 7, p. 87 at the end; Krey, p. 16–18; Rüping/Jerouschek (supra note 51), side note 29–35, 79–82; Eb. Schmidt (supra note 60, p. 93.

242 v. Hippel, p. 90; Krey, Interrogational Torture Vol. II (supra note 152), p. 16, 17; Rüping/Jerouschek, side note 82 with further reference.

243 Fried, p. 277, 278; Krey, p. 16, 17; Rüping/Jerouschek, side note 82.

244 See text above, Chapter Four IX 2 b, Firstly with footnote 214.

Germany took place. Here, autonomous town statutes were carried out including even criminal law.
a) However, in the High Middle Ages, such town statutes had not yet entered into the use of death penalty and interrogational torture. Rather, only after such use of cruel instruments in criminal proceedings had taken place in the northern Italian cities

– being role models for **German cities** at that time – ,

also the latter implemented death penalty and torture.
Such brutal development in **Italy** occurred since the 13th century. The reason for this may primarily have been the dramatic rise of urban mass crime, mostly committed by members of the lower social classes and poor newcomers to the city. Those offenders were subjected to a brief and dashing criminal trial.[245]
Later, **German** cities adopted the use of torture and capital punishment along the line of the aforesaid development in northern Italy, however not until the end of the 13th century/beginning of the 14th.[246] Here again, the main reason for such brutalisation of criminal law and criminal proceedings was the fight against urban mass crime committed by members of the lower social classes (in German then also called *"rand-ständige schädliche Leute"*, meaning marginal and antisocial elements) as well as traveling folk (in German *"fahrendes Volk"*).[247]
b) Indeed, the development of autonomous Town Statutes during the rise of German Cities took place in the High **Middle Ages**, namely since the end of the 11th century/beginning of the 12th. But this did not result in the rise of the *"Peinliches Strafrecht"* striking **life and limb** associated with the "Inquisitionsprozess" *ex officio* with brutal use of torture already in the course of **such era**. Rather, not until the **Late Middle Ages** that terrible misdevelopment took place resulting in the increasing rise of bloodthirsty, inhuman, and brutal criminal law as well as criminal proceedings.

---

245 v. Hippel, p. 89, 90, 94; Krey, p. 15, 16; Rüping/Jerouschek, side note 40–43, 81, 82; Wesel (supra note 1), side note 237.

246 Krey, Interrogational Torture Vol. II, p. 18; Rüping/Jerouschek, side note 53, 69, 78, 79, 81; Eb. Schmidt, p. 91, 92; Wesel, side note 236, 237.

247 See supra note 246.

Chapter Five: **A brief Outlook for the Late Middle Ages**

As far as the Early Middle Ages und the High Middle ages are concerned, the publication at hand may have shown that the frequent designation of the Middle Ages as **Dark Ages** is inappropriate. This in particular is true from a criminal law standpoint when you look at indicators such as **death penalty** and torture.[248] **42**

Here, in addition the issue **witch trials** as an important indicator for the characterization of an era is to be named. In this respect too, not until the Late Middle Ages you ought to designate the Middle Ages as Dark Ages.[249] Rather, as already repeatedly emphasized,[250] by no means the Early Middle Ages and the High Middle Ages should be named "Dark Ages". This is because firstly during the Early Middle Ages, the King and the Church neither have carried out criminal proceedings by use of torture and burning to death against witches and sorcerers nor have tolerated such perversions[251], and secondly because even the era of the High Middle Ages *"was not blemished by bloody witch hunting to any relevant extent"*.[252]

In contrast, in the course of the Late Middle Ages the legal development increasingly moved towards worrying criminal law and criminal proceedings. This assessment shall briefly be explained in the following text:

XII. Beginning and gradual Increase of the cruel "Inqisitionsprozess" ex officio characterized by Torture and Death Penalty during the Late Middle Ages

1. The Role of the Church

Still in the famous *Decretum Gratiani*, dated from the middle of the 12th century and then being the decisive collection of Canon Law by the monk and canon lawyer *Gratian*, there was a clear disapproval of interrogational torture.[253] Furthermore, in this spirit even the Council of 1215 under Pope **Innocent III** still waived the use of torture in case of persecuting heretics.[254] **43**

However, at the latest since the middle of the 13th century, in the course of developing the so-called canonical inquisitory process against heresy, the Church allowed the use of interrogational torture (Pope *Innocent IV*, 1252) and capital punishment by burning to death.[255]

So, the ecclesiastical refusal of **torture** and **capital punishment** following the time-honoured principle *"ecclesia non sitit sanguinem"* (the Church has no thirst for blood) was abandoned, and at the same time both cruel instruments were morally legitimated.

248 See text above Chapter Three VII 2, VIII 3, and Chapter Four IX 2 b, X, XI, all with further references.

249 Krey in Festschrift for da Costa Andrade (supra note 173), p. 423–426, 427 et seq.; Krey in Festschrift for Lindacher (supra note 6), p. 243 et seq., 247 et seq., 250; both with further references.

250 See supra note 248, 249.

251 Krey in Festschrift for Lindacher, p. 243–247, with further reference.

252 Krey in Festschrift für Lindacher, p. 247–249, with further references.

253 v. Hippel (supra note 56), p. 87 at the end, 88; Rüping/Jerouscheck (supra note 51), side note 30, 31, 81.

254 Eb. Schmidt (supra note 60), p. 93.

255 Thereto: Fried (supra note 78, p. 278; v. Hippel, p. 83 with footnote 4, 7, p. 86–90; Rüping/Jerouschek, side note 29–35, 79, 82.

2. The Role of northern Italian cities and German ones

44 In this context, the Pope referred to the fact that northern Italian cities, as mentioned above,[256] have used such torture since the beginning of the 13th century as "useful instrument" in the fight against urban mass crime.[257]
Later on, more precisely since the end of the 13th century, also German cities pursuant to the example of those northern Italian cities adopted the use of torture and **death penalty** in fighting urban mass crime.[258]

3. Beginning of bloodthirsty Witch Trials

45 In the course of the Late Middle Ages, trials for heresy more and more have been replaced by witch trials. Particularly during the last century of the Late Middle Ages (the 15th), there were witch hunts to a certain extent.[259] However, such cases of witch hunting were far from the monstrous waves of witch trials which occurred in the first two centuries of the Early Modern Age (the 16th and 17th); compared to such waves, previous witch trials were no mass phenomenon (*Wesel*).[260]
Rather, as the author has already stated in previous publications,[261] the **monstrous waves of witch trials,** in total resulting in **many tens of thousands dead**, took place during the first two centuries (the 16th and 17th) of the Early Modern Age,[262] more precisely: primarily in the course of the second half of the 16th century, and additionally in the 17th century during the thirties and sixties. Here, we should not forget that at that time most of the accused in witch trials were subjected to atrocious torture and at the end to the terrible death penalty by **burning.**

4. The Role of the German Territorial Princes

46 In the light of the mentioned cruel persecution of heretics by the Church, using torture and death penalty at the latest since the middle of the 13th century, and of the bloody persecution of urban mass crime by the German cities since the 14th century, the German Territories as well step by step established territorial criminal law, allowing torture and capital punishment.[263]
In this context, it should be recalled that since the first half of the 13th century the German Territorial Princes had wrested nearly the complete penal power from the German King/Emperor: Nobody less than the famous German Emperor *Frederic II of Hohenstaufen*, also King of Sicily, being under pressure by the German Princes, has 1232 confirmed the remarkable *"Statutum in favorem principum"* (statute in favor

---

256 See text above, Chapter Four, III 3 a.

257 v. Hippel, p. 89, 94; Rüping/Jerouschek, side note 40 et seq., 43, 81, 82; Wesel (supra note 1), side note 237; also see: Krey, Interrogational Torture Vol. II (supra note 152), p. 15, 16; Krey in Festschrift for da Costa Andrade (supra note 173), p. 423 et seq. with footnote 11.

258 Rüping/Jerouschek, side note 53, 69, 78, 81; Eb. Schmidt, p. 91, 92; Wesel (supra note 1), side note 236, 237.

259 Fried, p. 482; Jerouschek, Juristische Schulung (JuS, i.e. a German Law Journal), 1995, p. 576, 580; in addition see: Decker (supra note 224), p. 32 et seq., 35 et seq.; Frenschkowski (supra note 224), p. 22, 23, 119–121; Gaskill (supra note 224), p. 34–40, 66, 83.

260 Wesel, side note 261; already see Krey in Festschrift for Lindacher (supra note 6), p. 250.

261 Krey, Von Zauberern und Hexen. Rechtshistorische Betrachtungen, in Festschrift for Kristian Kühl (Tübingen), 2014, p. 19, 36 et seq., 39–44; Krey, About Magicians and Witches. Reflections on Legal History. The Early Modern Age (from the 16th until the 18th Century) as a Janus-faced Era ..., in: Festschrift for Gerhard Wolf (Frankfurt/Oder), 2018; Krey, Interrogational Torture, Vol. II (supra note 152), p. 30–36.

262 Rüping/Jerouschek, side note 145.

263 Rüping/Jerouschek, side note 82 at the end; Wesel, side note 237, 240. Also see Krey, Interrogational Torture Vol. II, p. 18, 19.

of the German princes). Here, the power of criminal law was delegated to the German territorial rulers, shortly later also the power of criminal legislation.[264]

5. The "Sachsenspiegel"

Even the famous *"Sachsenspiegel"*, written down by Knight *Eike von Repgow* around 1230[265] and subsequently becoming the most influential compendium of German Law, outlined several criminal offences threatened by death penalty,[266] such as murder, breaking the public peace by violence,[267] black magic, and theft. **47**

XIII. Hexenbulle and Hexenhammer: Major Blots with strong Impact on the Waves of Witch Trials during the first two Centuries of the Early Modern Age

At the End of the Late Middle Ages which had opened the floodgates to the *"Inquisitionsprozess"* characterized by **death penalty** and interrogational **torture**, things got even worse: In the eighties of the 15th century two major blots with strong influence on the use of such instruments had been published, namely the *"Hexenbulle"* (1484) and the *"Hexenhammer"* (1486/87); in this respect some brief remarks shall serve for clarification.[268] **48**

1. The Papal Bull *"Summis Desiderantes"* (in German *"Hexenbulle"* i.e. bull on witches)

This shameful sorry effort firstly had authorized the Inquisitor *Heinrich Kramer (Institoris)* to carry out witch hunts within the territory of the Holy Roman Empire of the German Nation. Secondly the Papal Bull ordered by apostolic authority that *Kramer's* activities as Inquisitor must not be obstructed. And thirdly the Bull accepted such delusions like *coitus cum diabolo* and black magic *(maleficium)* as being criminal witchcraft. So, the Pope gave his ecclesiastical authority to the witch hunting.[269] **49**

2. Kramer's combat writing "Malleus Maleficarum" ("Hexenhammer" i.e. witch hammer)

Soon after having been accredited as Inquisitor by the Pope, the Dominican *Kramer* carried out witch hunts in the diocese of Brixen. Here, he opened extensive investigations and thereby committed serious breaches of the law. Thus, the Bishop of Brixen, *Golser*, suspended that witch hunting and chased away *Kramer*. In doing so, *Golser* expressed doubts as to *Kramer's* mental sanity.[270] In order to prevent future resistance and to impose a comprehensive and merciless persecution of witchcraft, *Kramer* wrote down a combat writing entitled *Malleus Maleficarum (Hexenhammer)*, published in 1486/87. This devilish sorry effort/concoction particularly deals with the following issues:[271] **50**

The demon and the witch/sorcerer, in addition the appearance of witchcraft/sorcery.

---

264 Wesel, side note 206, 240. Regarding Frederic II also see: van. Eickels, Friedrich II (1212–12150) ... in: Schneidmüller/Weinfurter (editors), Die deutschen Herrscher des Mittelalters. Historische Portraits von Heinrich I. bis Maximilian I. (919–1519), 2003, p. 293 et seq., 306, 307.

265 Eike von Repgow, Der Sachsenspiegel, published by Clausdieter Schott, 1984.

266 Thereto: Rüping/Jerouschek (supra note 51), side note 54–57; Wesel (supra note 1), side note 220, 236.

267 As regards peace breaking see text above Chapter Four, XI 1.

268 Thereto in detail and with further references Krey in Festschrift for Manuel da Costa Andrade (supra note 173), p. 428–436.

269 Krey, p. 428–430 with further references and relevant **quotes from the "Hexenbulle"**.

270 Krey, p. 430 et seq. with further references and relevant **quotes from the "Hexenhammer"**.

271 See supra note 270.

Chapter Five: A brief Outlook for the Late Middle Ages

The "Kriminalkodex" (criminal code), covering methods of exterminating witches/ sorcerers, namely through the merciless terror of witch trials by using torture and capital punishment.
All of this firstly was a document of psychopathic misogyny as well as pathologically absurd delusions, and secondly – even worse – to a great extent the **basis** for the horror of witch trials in the course of the 16th and 17th century. At the same time, the *Hexenhammer* also was a decisive reason für the bloodthirsty **criminal justice in general** during such centuries. But that is another issue.